Getting On

ALAN BENNETT

FABER AND FABER
3 Queen Square
London

First published in 1972
by Faber and Faber Limited
3 Queen Square London WC1
Printed in Great Britain by
Latimer Trend & Co Ltd Plymouth
All rights reserved

ISBN 0 571 09941 6 (paper covered edition)
ISBN 0 571 09939 4 (hard bound edition)

CONDITIONS OF SALE

To KEITH

Characters

GEORGE OLIVER, M.P.
GEOFF PRICE
POLLY OLIVER
BRIAN LOWTHER, M.P.
ENID BAKER
ANDY OLIVER
MRS. BRODRIBB

Voices off:
Two children, a boy of eight, a girl of four

The play is set in London.
The time is the present.

Getting On opened at the Queen's Theatre on 14th October 1971.
The cast was as follows:

GEORGE OLIVER, M.P.	Kenneth More
POLLY OLIVER	Gemma Jones
BRIAN LOWTHER, M.P.	Brian Cox
ENID BAKER	Mona Washbourne
GEOFF PRICE	Sebastian Graham-Jones
ANDY OLIVER	Keith Skinner
MRS. BRODRIBB	Edna Doré

Directed by Patrick Garland

Designed by Julia Trevelyan Oman

Lighting by Joe Davis

Author's Note

The text here printed differs in some respects from that first presented at the Queen's Theatre. That version had been clumsily cut without my presence or permission and some small additions made: the jokes were largely left intact while the serious content of the play suffered.

I have removed the additions and largely restored the cuts. This makes the text overlong. But in the event of further productions I would ask that the play be cut with an eye to its seriousness as well as its humour. Otherwise it becomes a complacent light comedy with sad and sentimental moments.

The play was originally entitled *A Serious Man*.

ACT ONE

The play is set in the basement or the ground floor of an Edwardian house, of which the kitchen and living-room run into one another. The kitchen is at the rear of the stage. The outside door is upstage and there is another door downstage which goes upstairs. Also downstage left is a large Victorian overmantel mirror, which George frequently addresses. There is much white paint, and the house has an airy good feeling to it ... not cluttered Victoriana. Nevertheless, there are a lot of objects around, furniture, glasses, pictures. A collage of children's drawings on the wall, photographs, Mr. Heath, 'Private Eye' covers. A red election rosette, haphazard, not artistic. A string of onions, a pan stand, some stripped pine. But not new looking. Fairly worn. It shouldn't look particularly smart or trendy.

There is a child crying upstairs.

GEORGE OLIVER, M.P. *enters.*

He is a man of about forty, rather glamorous once, now a bit florid, worn, running to fat. He wears quite good clothes, but they don't hang well on him. He smokes cheroots.

His voice, originally northern, is now a pretty nondescript educated voice, but his accent thickens when angry or passionate. He is a deeply misanthropic man, hence his jokes.

GEORGE: If I were to be taken and pinioned for hours at a time in a shuddering, jerking box of steel and glass, lights flashed in my eyes, fumes blown up my nose and gas pumped into my lungs, if this were to be done by the Chinese, then I should be the subject of stern leaders in *The Times* and the righteous anger of the *Daily Express*. Yet I submit to this treatment of my own free will. I do it every week and it's called driving down to London. Hello.

(*During this speech* GEOFF *has entered from the stairs door, and hangs about behind him.* GEOFF *is nineteen, handsome in a Pre-Raphaelite way and very thin.*)

I thought you were Polly.

GEOFF: (*who looks at himself as if not entirely certain he isn't*): N-o-o.

GEORGE: Who are you? No. Don't tell me. You could be one of several people. You aren't the man from the central heating, or the man who comes to mend the washing machine. Both almost daily visitors. Perhaps you are another unemployed actor. Several leading lights in the National Theatre have not been ashamed to plunge their feather dusters through our accumulated possessions. Indeed, that is one of the reasons I don't go to the theatre: it's hard to believe in Pastor Manders when you knew him first as a somewhat below average window cleaner. And if not an actor, what?

GEOFF: The marble, I . . .

GEORGE: A supply teacher perhaps. My son has bitten Miss Gainsborough's leg again? Or from the Portobello Road with a new addition to our already definitive collection of stripped pine?

GEOFF: I brought the marble.

GEORGE: Marble?

GEOFF: They were clearing out this old bakery in Kentish Town and Polly . . . your wife . . . thought the slabs would come in useful, somewhere.

GEORGE: Somewhere. Look around this room . . . I'm sorry, I don't know your name.

GEOFF: Geoff.

GEORGE: Look around this room, Geoff. Can you see anywhere where marble might come in useful? Do you see any surface not adequately covered, anywhere in fact where marble might come in handy?

GEOFF: Not off-hand, no.

GEORGE: No. And the only reason I can think of why my wife should be picking up the odd marble slab is that with her customary foresight and economy she thinks it will come in handy for a good gravestone for me.

GEOFF: I don't think so.

GEORGE: Is she upstairs?

GEOFF: She's just putting the children to sleep.

GEORGE: Humanely, I hope. Oh, shut up. I've caught this mood of relentless facetiousness from the car radio. Have you noticed that the BBC keeps its silliest programmes, and its jokiest announcers, for those times in the morning and evening when people are on their way to and from *work*. It's very significant. Why should the BBC choose those times to cover the land in a pall of fatuity? What is it about work that we have to be hurried to and from it by drivelling idiots? I tell you what I think, I think it's an indication of profound malaise in the social structure.

GEOFF: I'd never thought of that.

GEORGE: Is that tea you're making?

GEOFF: Yes.

GEORGE: That's not the teapot. There's the teapot.

GEOFF: Yes. Sorry.

GEORGE: That is an appliance for forcing beef tea down the noses of unsuspecting invalids. It hasn't quite found its place yet.

GEOFF: It's nice. You've got lots of nice things.

GEORGE: We have so many things that by the law of averages some of them must be nice.

(POLLY *enters by the stairs door left. She is thirtyish, attractive, perceptibly younger than* GEORGE. *Harassed. Scatterbrained, or deliberately giving that impression, but not stupid. She is carrying a pile of children's clothes, or one or two of the children's paintings. She should always be doing something about the house, finding odd jobs to do. She never wastes a minute.*)

POLLY: It *is* you. James said it was you and I said it was time he went to sleep.

CHILD'S VOICE: Dad. Dad. Dad.

(*She shouts up the stairs.*)

POLLY: No, it isn't George. It's the television.

CHILD'S VOICE: Will you come up and see me?

POLLY: No, I can't. Not now. Read your reading book. This is George, my husband. This is Geoff . . . I never asked your other name.

GEOFF: Price.

POLLY: Price. By rights it's an old-fashioned inhaler. I can't think what to do with it.

GEOFF: Flowers?

POLLY: Flowers, I suppose, but I always thinks that's a bit of a defeat. James has been using it as a rocket launcher. I suppose it will come in somewhere. Sit down, Geoff.

GEOFF: Can't I help?

POLLY: I'll see to it. How were the dark satanic mills?

GEORGE: Rather nice today. I saw Nelly and Sam who send their regards. The Town Hall do was bloody. I said my piece for Granada. And I saw a falcon on the Motorway. (*To* GEOFF.) Sit down, sit down, for goodness' sake.

POLLY: Are you wanting anything to eat? We had ours with the children.

GEORGE: No. I ate on the Motorway. At the "Grid n'Griddle". I had ham n'eggs. And now I've got 'ndigestion. Oh, and I ran into McMasters.

POLLY: In Manchester? Which cup would you like?

GEOFF: I'm easy. Any.

POLLY: Would you like A View of Lowestoft, a Masonic mug from Salford, or The Revd. E. S. Clough, Twenty-Five Years at Scotney Road Chapel, Pudsey?

GEOFF: Yes, that one.

GEORGE: There's not much to choose except that one's chipped, one's cracked and the other you can't get your finger through the handle.

POLLY: Scones. They're home-made.

GEOFF: If I lived here I should get fat.

GEORGE: He said I could go back to Oxford any time I wanted.

POLLY: That's nice to know, anyway. Lovely and thin, George used to be, just like you.

GEORGE: I don't think I was ever quite as thin as that.

POLLY: I wouldn't care about you getting fatter if you were getting jollier. People are thinner now, aren't they. Young people. Younger people, I mean. It's the right foods.

GEORGE: We never had any oranges during the war. You won't remember the war, of course.

GEOFF: No.

GEORGE: People don't seem to, nowadays. I don't suppose you were even born when it ended.

GEOFF: No. Not by a long way.

POLLY: It's funny. One meets more and more people who weren't. There didn't used to be any, and now one meets them all the time.

GEORGE: I remember the end of the war. In fact I remember the actual war.

GEOFF: That must be great.

GEORGE: Yes, it is.

(*Pause.*)

GEOFF: Did you fight at all?

GEORGE: No. I wasn't old enough.

GEOFF: It must be awful to have, you know, your earliest memories . . . you know, sort of seared by it.

GEORGE: Yes. I was evacuated to Harrogate . . . and that was a bit . . . searing. Were you . . . seared at all, Polly?

(POLLY *pointedly ignores him.*)

More tea, Geoff?

GEOFF: It's the German side of it that interests me.

GEORGE: We weren't so much interested in the Germans as bitterly opposed to them.

GEOFF: I collect one or two things . . . badges, things like that.

POLLY: Really? I'll keep my eyes open. I often see odd bits of things when I'm on my travels. I'm not sure we don't have a bit of shrapnel upstairs. A buzz bomb fell near us at Stanmore. Would you be interested in that?

(*A horn sounds outside.*)

GEOFF: That would be marvellous.

POLLY: It's just a jagged bit of metal really, but it would be nice if someone had it who really appreciated it . . . for what it is. I've never been able to find a use for it.

(*A horn sounds again, more angrily.*)

GEORGE: All right, all right. I'm double parked. You can't even park outside your own house.

(*He goes out by the street door.*)

POLLY: George is an M.P.

15

GEOFF: What sort?

POLLY: Guess.

GEOFF: Cons . . .

POLLY: No.

GEOFF: Sorry.

POLLY: I'm not offended.

GEOFF: It's just that . . . he has . . . a look about him . .

POLLY: That's not party, that's politics. He's been up in his constituency holding a surgery. Where people come and tell him their troubles.

GEOFF: What sort of thing? Troubles?

GEORGE: He'd got miles of room.

POLLY: All sorts.

GEORGE: The council's demolishing their houses, the Ministry withholding their pensions, benefits, compensation, ejection. The load of bitterness and despair people hump about with them you'd be amazed.

POLLY: It's a very poor constituency. He was lucky to get it . . . I mean . . .

GEORGE: Not really. Poor. At least not many. It's the ones who've gone to the wall. I had a woman in today who believes that her husband, an unemployed fitter, is having an affair with the Queen. And that the Household Cavalry had her under constant watch.

POLLY: Why the Household Cavalry?

GEORGE: Why the Queen?

POLLY: Poor soul. What did you say?

GEORGE: We agreed that the best thing for me to do was to ask the Duke of Edinburgh to have a quiet word with Her Majesty and when she'd gone I had a quiet word with the Mental Health Officer. Poor bugger. Then there was an enormous West Indian woman who said the people next door kept poisoning her cat and the police wouldn't listen to her. I didn't do anything about that at all.

POLLY: There ought to be some way of stopping them wasting your time.

GEORGE: That's why they land up with me, because nobody else has been prepared to waste their time. They just get passed on. They can't get into the army, they can't get out of the army, the wife's gone off with the kids, the kids have gone into a home, a policeman's hit them over the head. Then some people come just because it's free and they want to talk to somebody and they know it's their right. I'm quite sure there are seventy-year-old ladies who line up at the ante-natal clinic because they'd feel cheated if they didn't.

(GEOFF *is a good listener and laughs at all* GEORGE's *more obvious jokes.*)

The words Member of Parliament still have prestige though, extraordinary. One phone call and officials are scuttling about all over the place.

GEOFF: That's great.

GEORGE: There are still people who stink, did you know that? They sit there on the other side of the table in Sam's airless little office and they stink of muck and squalor and filth and despair. They're just clinging on to the bare face of life. Sorry. Shop.

POLLY: I'm just trying to think what else there is to do. Is electricity in your line, because there's the landing light. I ought to have asked Captain Oates to do it.

GEOFF: Who?

POLLY: Captain Oates. We call him, anyway. He was an electrician who came to do the bathroom. One day he went off saying, "I'm just going out. I may be quite a time." And he never came back. So George christened him Captain Oates.

(GEOFF *is perplexed and silent.*)

Sorry. Captain Oates was someone who went with Captain Scott.

(GEOFF *smiles, but is still uncomprehending.*)

The first man to . . .

GEORGE: The first Englishman——

POLLY: The first Englishman to get to the North——

GEORGE: South.

POLLY: South Pole. This Captain Oates was with him. He had a bad leg or something, and was holding them up so one night he went out of the tent saying, "I'm just going outside. I may be some time." When really they all knew he wasn't going to come back.

GEOFF: Oh.
    (*He tries to force a laugh.*)
GEORGE: Though it's my belief he may have been going for a
    particularly long slash.
POLLY: Anyway, that's why we called the plumber Captain Oates.
GEOFF: I thought you said it was the electrician.
POLLY: It was.
    (*Pause.*)
GEOFF: You must think I'm thick.
GEORGE: No. It's just a fact. You know it or you don't.
GEOFF: You both know it, though.
GEORGE: So? It's like knowing about cars or the times of trains.
    Facts. Nothing to do with intelligence. Of course I'm not
    saying you're not thick. Only that that doesn't prove it. I
    could well do without knowing about Captain Oates. Useless
    facts swilling about the brain. Could all be drained off and I
    should be none the wiser. Or none the stupider.
    (*A crash and crying from upstairs.*)
    Look out, I can hear Thompson and Bywaters. Our two
    children at present on licence from Strangeways. James
    seven . . .
POLLY: Eight.
GEORGE: And Elizabeth, three?
    (POLLY *creeps to the door and listens.*)
POLLY: Go to sleep, love. No, he's not. You're not to come down.
    (*Sounds of children coming downstairs.* GEORGE *goes to the door
    and flings it open.*)
GEORGE: No, young man. Back you go. You've no business to be
    out of bed. Up, up, up.
    (GEORGE *goes upstairs.*)
POLLY: They are demons. Have you got a flat?
GEOFF: Sort of.
POLLY: Do you live with someone. I mean not live with "live
    with", I mean——
GEOFF: Yes. In Notting Hill. We have this house. It's owned by
    some anarchists. I suppose it's a sort of commune really . . .
    we're always borrowing each other's butter anyway.
    (POLLY *should be active throughout this, clearing up tea things,*

backwards and forwards between the kitchen and living-room,
so that sometimes she misses his comments and he hers.)
We started off trying to set up a small anarchist community
but people wouldn't obey the rules.

POLLY: I suppose you think we're very corrupt.

GEOFF: No. Are you?

POLLY: All this . . . property, possessions. Politics.

GEOFF: Not this sort of stuff. This isn't really possessions, is it?

POLLY: Isn't it?

GEOFF: No. Most people wouldn't want this sort of stuff, anyway.
Do I make you nervous?

POLLY: What? No. No.

(*But he does.* GEORGE *comes down.*)

GEORGE: He wants a banana and she wants a cup of tea. How
many sugars?

POLLY: It varies.

GEORGE: How many sugars.

(*Unidentifiable shout.*)

Seven! Seven.

POLLY: How did you take up . . . sort of . . . doing nothing?

GEOFF: I wasn't much good at school. I got rheumatic fever when
I was ten, and I got behindhand. I went to a special school
for a bit.

(GEORGE *is now going upstairs again with the tea.*)

Then I kept being off school and never really got the hang of
it again.

(POLLY *is in the kitchen.*)

There was a group of us. We just used to sit at the back of
the class and wank.

POLLY: Was it a comprehensive school then?

GEOFF: And I reckoned I could do that just as well at home. I
went round Art School for a bit, but I didn't reckon that
much either. Are you Sagittarius?

POLLY: Me? Why? I always forget. December 14. I generally have
to look it up.

GEOFF (*nodding*): Sagittarius.

POLLY: How do you know?

GEOFF: Vibes, I suppose.

POLLY: It's dogs and sport, isn't it, Sagittarius? Not really me.

GEOFF: I sussed this Libra bird on the Tube last week and she'd never opened her mouth.

POLLY: What's George then, if you're so good at guessing?

GEOFF: Leo.

POLLY: What are you? July 30. Yes, he is. You are Leo, aren't you? Fancy Geoff knowing that.

GEORGE: It's rubbish.

GEOFF: It isn't, you know.

(*They are about to start and argue, but* GEOFF *thinks better of it.*)

Where is this plug?

POLLY: In the cistern cupboard. Mind you don't get a shock.

(*He opens the stairs door,* GEORGE *hears the kids coming and pushes him aside.*)

GEORGE: All right, it's very nice of you to bring the cup down, thank you. But, James, if I catch you out of bed once more there'll be no Jugoslavia. Right? "Suffer the little children to come unto me." You might know Jesus wasn't married. (GEOFF *goes upstairs.*)

He says you didn't read with him.

POLLY: There wasn't time. Besides I don't understand this new system. There I am going C-A-T and they don't do it like that any more.

GEORGE: Will you hear my words?

POLLY: What for?

GEORGE: That television. Here. . . . Skip the first bit, I'm going to rewrite that . . . burble, burble, burble . . . ours is still a society in which we throw people into the dustbin, some sooner, some later. We chuck some people in at fifteen, we chuck others in at sixty-five. Our society is one that produces a colossal amount of rubbish. Litter, junk, waste. Yes?

POLLY: The leftovers.

GEORGE: The leftovers. And in among the leftovers are people. We waste people. The best society—I think a socialist society —is one in which fewest people are wasted.

POLLY: Elizabeth's bottom's cleared up a treat.

(GEORGE *should be only half saying the speech, and altering it as he goes through, while* POLLY *doesn't give it much attention either.*)

GEORGE: Somehow society must be kept open, open at every level so that there are always options . . .

(GEORGE *sits down—and winces.*)

Oh, sod it, what have I sat on?

(*He fetches out a crumpled, brightly painted construction.*)

POLLY: It's The Ark. James was very proud of it.

GEORGE: Egg boxes. Always egg boxes. Miss Gainsborough has pushed the potentialities of egg boxes beyond man's wildest dreams. I reckon she must be getting a retainer from the Egg Marketing Board.

POLLY: It's true. All schools are the same.

GEORGE: What I want to know is when they take the crucial step from egg boxes to differential calculus. I believe that some people are better than others, better not because they're cleverer or more cultivated or God knows—(*He laughs*)— because they're better off, but——

POLLY: Are you going to do that?

GEORGE: What?

(POLLY *imitates his mid-sentence laugh.*)

I might. Why?

POLLY: Oh, nothing.

(GEORGE *is nonplussed. He repeats the sequence without laughing.*)

You didn't laugh.

GEORGE: You said . . .

POLLY: No. I liked it.

GEORGE: It's a kind of grace, I think. The chosen few. If you can't produce such people because I'm not sure they're born not made, if you can't produce them, then what you can do, and this is where socialism comes in, what you can do, is to show such people to themselves, to link them up.

POLLY: I don't think Miss Gainsborough takes much notice of James. When I spoke to her last week she had to think before she even knew who he was.

GEORGE: Not surprising if there are thirty-odd kids in the class. Anyway what does it matter? He is thick. We have got ourselves a thick child.

POLLY: Why should he be thick. I was a bright girl.

GEORGE: Heredity isn't a law of the land. If one only knew beforehand what one's children were going to be like. One ought to be able to see a trailer.

"Pause before you enter here
  Lest from this womb a child appear.
  Matchless he in face and skin
  Fair of hair and clean of limb
  But let not your mind your senses rob,
  For he will be a stupid slob."

POLLY: You laugh. If Andy were my son . . .

GEORGE: Ah, but Andy is not your son, and Andy, thank God, has brains. Brains and beauty, the only untaxable inheritance. He never had any special treatment and look at him. An advertisement for the comprehensive system, brighter than ever I was and beautiful with it. I don't suppose you've seen him?

POLLY: He was in at tea-time, just for a minute.

GEORGE: Even now touching up some respectable girl in the Classic, Baker Street.

POLLY: So we can't just abandon him.

GEORGE: Andy?

POLLY: James.

(*Pause.*)

I think he ought to go to Freshfields.

GEORGE: He is not going to Freshfields.

(*They have plainly had this conversation before.*)

Saunders Road, even with Miss Gainsborough is a very . . .

POLLY: I'm not having his whole life sacrificed to your principles . . .

GEORGE: His whole life. The kid is seven.

POLLY: Eight. You don't even know how old your own child is. Mozart was practically dead by the time he was his age. And why is it always the kids who suffer for the principle? Why is it, it's when it comes to schooling we always have to run up the Red Flag. Education with socialists, it's like sex, all right so long as you don't have to pay for it.

GEORGE: I am not having him educated with a load of shrill-voiced

Tory boys to buy him advancement which at the moment his talents do not appear to merit.

POLLY: Merit. How can you talk about merit. At seven.

GEORGE: Eight. I don't know what you're bothering about. The first sound he learns to imitate is that of a police klaxon. He is capable of detecting the subtlest distinctions in bodywork and performance. At the moment all indications are that we have brought into the world a tiny used car dealer.

POLLY: You see, even about something like this, you can't be serious. It's jokes, isn't it. Scoring. You are condemning him to . . .

GEORGE (*irritated by* POLLY'*s intrusion*): I know what I'm condemning him to better than you do. I mean I had a state education.

POLLY: State education? You?

GEORGE: I went to a grammar school. (*Exits.*)

POLLY: Grammar school! Founded about 400 B.C. and wearing long blue frocks, some grammar school!
(*The lights change to indicate the time has changed. Possibly a child cries again upstairs as the stage is dark.* GEORGE *enters with* BRIAN LOWTHER, M.P., *better dressed, better spoken but otherwise little different from* GEORGE.)

BRIAN: I was expecting another three o'clock do tonight. (*Yawns.*) I reckon you must all be losing heart.

GEORGE: What I don't understand about you, Brian . . . what's the matter?

BRIAN: I think I must have . . . (*He lifts his shoe.*)

GEORGE: Yes, you have. It's that bloody dalmatian.

BRIAN: Better hop outside and get rid of it. (*Steps outside.*)

GEORGE: It's always here that's what gets me.
Why is it always us? Why does it always have to do its No. 2's at No. 17?

BRIAN: It doesn't happen in Australia. Did you know that? When I went on that extremely boring parliamentary mission to that God-forsaken . . .
(*He comes back.*)
. . . albeit, let it be said Commonwealth country, the thing that impressed me most, lifeguards apart, was the sweetness of the streets.

23

GEORGE: I reckon it's sussed we're the only Socialists in the street. Question that dog closely and you'll find it reads the *Daily Express*. If I ever catch it dropping its nasty canine britches round here again I'll kick it into the middle of next week. And her as well, Mrs. Frederick Brodribb.

BRIAN: Ah ah. She sounds like a supporter of the Conservative and Unionist Party. That's right. Shove the kettle on. I'm exhausted by that gruelling confrontation.

GEORGE: You're so sensible in many respects but when you actually get down to it, you're just as bad as the rest of them.

BRIAN: That's right.

GEORGE: I mean. Let's be clear what we are talking about. We are talking about the kind of class you can see any day of the week, shambling through Leeds or Nottingham, or Sheffield, shepherded by some broken-down, underpaid, defeated old man of forty-five. The class despises him. The passers-by pity him. He is the secondary school-teacher walking his charges to the baths, traipsing them through art galleries, trying not to see as they shove people off the pavement and make grabs at each other's balls.

BRIAN: I don't think you can blame that on Mrs. Thatcher.

GEORGE: And on the other side we have a nice little crocodile of grey-flannelled boys with little pink caps and high middle-class voices going home to Children's Hour and Ballet Shoes and Noel Streatfeild. Which is very nice. Except that these others, they're going home to get their own teas in Peabody Buildings. They're going home to margarine adverts and the *TV Times*, and some of them, quite certainly, a fuck. At thirteen.

BRIAN: Bully for them.

GEORGE: All right. I know I'm being boring. That's quintessential Toryism. Any trace of passion or concern, they say you're being boring.

BRIAN: All right. I went to public school, of course. But looking back on it I think it may have been Borstal. I was taught by a succession of teachers all of whom seemed to have lost one or other of their limbs. It was cold, the food was disgusting, there was a great deal of what seemed to me entirely unnecessary running about and the sanitation was such as to make me a lifelong convert to constipation. And I would not send my worst enemy to public school. BUT if there are parents who are prepared to spend money on educating their children in such places . . . I am not going to stop them any more than I would stop them spending their money on power boats or go-kart racing or any other sophisticated way of throwing money down the drain. It's a question of freedom.

GEORGE: It is not a question of freedom, it's a question of justice. (POLLY *comes downstairs, still carrying a pile of children's clothes, and wearing, as the simplest method of carrying it, a space helmet.*)

(BRIAN *kisses her, and she sniffs at him appreciatively.*)

POLLY: I was hoping he'd bring you back.

GEORGE: That flaming dog has messed on our steps again. It's the one species I wouldn't mind seeing vanish from the face of the earth. I wish they were like the White Rhino—six of them left in the Serengeti National Park, and all males. Do you know what dogs are? They're those beer-sodden soccer fans piling out of coaches in a layby, yanking out their cocks without a blush and pissing against the wall thirty-nine in a row. I can't stand it.

POLLY: Question is whether you hate the coach party because they're like the dogs or hate the dogs because they're like the coach party.

GEORGE: I hate them all. Where did you get that suit from?

BRIAN: It's old. I got it when I was in the army. Chester, I think.

GEORGE: Why don't my suits look like that?

BRIAN: Taste.

GEORGE: Not taste. Nothing that implies one cares. It looks like it's grown on you, that suit. I want something like that, bred in the bone, without anybody thinking I've paused before the mirror and *chosen* it. I want an honest suit of good broadcloth . . . whatever that is. I want to look like Sir Kenneth Clark or a well-to-do solicitor in a Scottish town or the head of an Oxford college. Such a suit as Montaigne might have worn, had he lived, or Marcus Aurelius.

BRIAN: And something wrong, that's the mark of real distinction: the tie too loosely knotted, a bit of dinner down the waistcoat.

POLLY: He's got that anyway.

BRIAN: You should go to my tailor.

GEORGE: There you are, you see. My tailor, my doctor, my dentist. Your servants. With me it's the tailor, the doctor, the dentist. They're not mine. And I'm not theirs. Oh, God, if it were only clothes though. Look at this dry pink plate of a face. Why didn't God give me a face on which the skin hangs in genial brown folds, the mouth is firm . . . but kindly . . . and with long large ears. Nearly every man of distinction has long ears.

(POLLY *and* BRIAN *involuntarily finger theirs.*)

BRIAN: In short you want them to look like one of us and be like one of them.

GEORGE: When I walk down the street I want people to think, "There goes a sadder and wiser man." Instead of which it's "Christ. He looks a slob." Must have a pee.

POLLY: Well, don't wake the children. George's trouble is . . . are you eating . . .

(BRIAN *shakes his head.*)

He's a socialist but he doesn't like people.

BRIAN: Nor do I, much.

POLLY: You're a conservative. You don't have to.

BRIAN: No.

POLLY: There'll doubtless be a bit of something tasty in the oven, cooked by the faithful Mrs. Minter. Oh, Brian, it's a nice life, yours.

BRIAN: I have an ordered life, if that's nice. All is order. Would you like some cake?

POLLY: I . . . would I like some cake? No. Why?

BRIAN: In the car there's a seed cake, a madeira cake, two dozen jam tarts, and various bunches of assorted flowers, stuff I've brought back from my constituency.

POLLY: Were you opening a fête?

BRIAN: Not especially. My constituency's run by a handful of big middle-class ladies. And I am their darling. Miss Cornfield, Miss Venables, Mrs. Strickland. They love me.

POLLY: I wish ours was. You never see any of the women, ever. And it's all beer and butties. All I ever get is black pudding and black looks.

BRIAN: I just wish I had the energy of middle-class women in middle age. They'd organized this sale of work. There they were. Sturdy-legged, freckled-forearmed, horny-elbowed ladies. And the sort of arms that fill with fat, flesh-coloured flesh their flowered frocks.

POLLY: And lots of straying shoulder straps.

BRIAN: Blood donors, cake makers, good mixers, stout old-fashioned cart-horses, ploughing through day after day. Flustered only by sex, and sometimes not even by that. I could do with even a tenth of the energy they devote to flower arrangement.

(GEORGE *can come back anywhere here.*)

POLLY: They're a vanishing breed.

BRIAN: No. You're a bit like that.

GEORGE: See!

BRIAN: But why, I kept wondering today. What drives the pistons? What is it that puts one firm-fleshed sensible-shoed leg in front of the other day after day after day? What thoughts do you think flood in as they ease lisle stockings down those massive legs? And in the decency of the bathroom slip into one of Arthur's old pyjama jackets?

POLLY: It's like me. Escaping boredom.

BRIAN: Boredom. They don't know the meaning of the word. And those firm capable hands. Fingers that can with equal facility bottle gooseberries, address envelopes, arrange peonies, bind wounds, decontaminate (in the event of a nuclear attack) an entire village, pray, pry and at life's end lie freckled and calm upon the sheets with no sense of life wasted or purpose lost. O fierce, foolish Tory ladies, I love you. Except that I, your Member of Parliament, your elected representative at the Palace of Westminster am an outrageous pouff.

GEORGE: Get on! Not outrageous at all. About as outrageous as St. Augustine.

POLLY: He wasn't, was he? The sly devil. I'm surprised they never twig.

BRIAN: No. I'm just an agreeable young man who knows how to behave. No, they don't twig. Mind you, I've caught one or two of the 1922 Committee eyeing me uneasily, lest I should suddenly launch myself on their vast pin-striped bottoms. "Can't have pouffs in the Conservative Party. No seat would be safe."

POLLY: I don't think they're human at all, half of them.

BRIAN: Who?

POLLY: The 1922 Committee.

GEORGE: No. A good test is whether you can imagine them on the lavatory. I reckon they just go in there, stand behind the door for five minutes then come out again . . . just to convince you they're like everybody else.

BRIAN: It's a good job I got my seat without having to go through the cattle market. Normally you're not considered worthy of the trust of the electorate unless you've gone under the yoke with one of those upper class land girls from the front page of *Country Life*. Your credentials are a brace of spoiled and flaxen-haired children, evidence that you have on at least two occasions hoisted yourself on to her massive thighs. Though quite how this makes one of more use to the Conservative Party I am at a loss to imagine. No. Give me a nice, clean, sad boy of nineteen any day.

GEORGE: Candidates will attend in company with their wives and/or boyfriends. That will be liberalism.

BRIAN: That's enough anyway. I can't stand talking about it. Some of them talk about nothing else. It's like making a career of being five foot eleven.

GEORGE: Brian, you see, is like me. What we both crave in life is order.

POLLY: Marriage and home is order.

BRIAN: Come on. Undies marinating in the basin, no nice cool places in the bed. And kids. There can't be order where there are children . . . children are anarchists, booby-trapping the stairs . . .

GEORGE: Oh, if it were only the stairs. One's whole life mined with affection and grief and remorse and ingratitude. Perhaps *that's* what's wrong with me . . . perhaps in the ninth year of

28

my second marriage . . .

POLLY: Tenth year.

GEORGE: Perhaps in the tenth year of my second marriage I realize
too late that I am homosexual by nature. Except that I don't
like men.

POLLY: You don't like anybody.

GEORGE: Look at Brian. He is still a free man. Look at me . . .
tethered like Gulliver by a thousand tiny ropes to every object
in this house. Festooned with the fruit of a hundred visits to
the Portobello Road, weighted down with jelly moulds, bread
crocks, brass, old photographs. Yes, and children. You're
right, they're part of it. Objects like the rest, except that
they've been manufactured on the premises, in this century,
in our lifetime and we haven't quite found a place for them
yet. But they're possessions and ornaments. And they've got
to be polished in order to do us credit.

POLLY: Here we go again.

GEORGE: Anyway, I can go back to Oxford any time I want.

ENID'S VOICE: Hello?

POLLY: Oh, God, it's Enid. What's she doing here?
(*She runs for the stairs door.*)

BRIAN: Who is it? Don't abandon me.
(GEORGE *also hides.*)
(ENID, POLLY's *mother, enters with a large canvas bag. She is a
jolly, slightly raffish lady of about sixty, made up in rather a
slapdash way, somewhat Bohemian.*)

ENID: Hello, anybody in? It's me. Oh!

BRIAN: My name's Lowther, a friend of George's. I'm his pair.
We've just been . . .

ENID: Come again.

BRIAN: In the house. Voting.

ENID: Oh! I'm Enid, her mother. Never a popular person with
my daughter, I'm afraid. She's doubtless just run upstairs?

BRIAN: No. She . . .

ENID: She generally does. Took the wrong turning somewhere in
childhood. Devoted to her father. Hates me. Of course she
was denied the breast. It always tells.
(*She has eventually put all her belongings down and holds out*

her hand.)

How do you do. Sorry about the paint stains. I've just been to my sex class . . . well, actually it's my life class but this term we're on the nude. We've got rather a nice young man posing at the moment. He's rather a dish. But, I suspect, a nancy. Like everybody else these days. Not that there's anything wrong in that. More power to his elbow, that's what I say.

(GEORGE *has come out of hiding and crept up behind her.*)

I say! There's a strange hand on my breast. I think I must be being interfered with.

(POLLY *comes back.*)

GEORGE: Hello, you lovely old Communist.

POLLY: George. Mother. For goodness' sake. That really is unnatural. George is the only person I know actually to be besotted with his mother-in-law. If everybody was like you, music-hall comedians would go out of business.

GEORGE: They have. We don't mind, do we, Enid?

ENID: No. We have a disgusting relationship. (*Kisses him.*) The nicest thing about being old, dear, is that you can do anything you like with a man and nobody thinks you're flirting.

GEORGE: This has cheered me up. But you never come on a Thursday.

ENID: I've got to go to the doctors tomorrow so I thought I'd come today *en route* from the Polytechnic. What're you depressed about?

POLLY: He's got nothing to be depressed about at all.

ENID: My daughter. A very understanding person. (*To* BRIAN.) Have you any children?

POLLY: He's not married.

ENID: He's quite capable of telling me that himself. He *is* a Member of Parliament. So domineering. Oh, Polly, look at your verbena toxicana. It's absolutely parched. And its requirements are minimal. That's why I chose it.

POLLY: I don't like cacti. They're the only plants I don't like.

ENID: It's not a cacti. It's a succulent. Give you a plant and it's like sending it to the salt mines. Come along now let's give you a drinkie. That's better. All gone. All gone.

POLLY: I've never been any good with cacti. They need expertise.

ENID: Expertise. One thimbleful of water every blue moon does not constitute expertise. Otherwise we should all be fellows of the Royal Horticultural Society, eh, Mr. Lowther?

GEORGE: Let's have a look at your masterpiece.

ENID: I'm not entirely happy with it. The shoulders are good, you see, but I've never quite got the hang of arms. Whereas Zoë, at the next easel, she's just the reverse. But rather fetching, don't you think?

GEORGE: I'll take it on trust.

ENID: And he will insist on not wearing a stitch. Zoë gets quite agitated. Normally, you see, they wear what I believe is called a posing pouch.

POLLY: Oh, Mother.

ENID: Don't you oh, Mother, me. I know we're not supposed to be interested at our age. Children always assume the sexual lives of their parents come to a grinding halt at their conception.

POLLY: But you're so *New Statesman* and old-fashioned about it. It proclaims your thirties upbringing.

ENID: If that's the only thing that proclaims my thirties upbringing I think I'm doing very nicely.

POLLY: We're all emancipated now.

ENID: Not in Stanmore we're not. Things are very different there. And it's all very well to sneer at the *New Statesman*, but in the thirties it was the only thing kept one sane. You're quite shy, aren't you?

BRIAN: Me? No.

ENID: I think you are. I know one thing. If I had my time over again I wouldn't have daughters. I'd have geraniums. At least geraniums are grateful. Where've I seen you before? Television. I can't remember what it was you were talking about. You never can on television, can you! More freedom was it, or more control? Something, anyway. I quite agree, though. Mind you, all we ever watch is the wrestling. I saw a lovely programme the other night. With badgers. No, dolphins. And the D. of Edinburgh. He says dolphins are quite intelligent. And very friendly. But then he's the D. of

Edinburgh so I suppose they would be.

BRIAN: I wish I'd kept my mouth shut.

ENID: Why? It seemed very sensible to me.

BRIAN: Anybody who stands up and says total freedom may not be a good thing is immediately swamped with appreciative letters from old ladies whose twin hobbies are prize cucumbers and the castration of sex offenders.

GEORGE: Exactly. You look round and find you've become right marker for the Awkward Squad . . . evangelists in belted raincoats, defeated prep schoolmasters, hard-mouthed ladies in gay hats.

BRIAN: Regimental Sergeant-Majors in the W.V.S.

GEORGE: It's the S.S., Save Society by Stopping Sex, Stupid Sods.

BRIAN: Opinions come in sets nowadays. You're either one of us or one of them. Like this.

(*He takes out a postcard.*)

POLLY: Nice postcard. Victoria Park Oswestry. There's no message.

BRIAN: No.

POLLY: Who sent it?

BRIAN: I don't know. Some lunatic.

POLLY: Can I have it?

(BRIAN *shrugs and* POLLY *puts it on the mantelpiece or sticks it in the corner of the mirror.*)

GEORGE: What is it you're off to the doctors for? If it's infectious don't tell me or I shall certainly get it.

ENID: I very much doubt it. Hot flushes, ladies' diseases, nothing I could possibly come out with in company.

GEORGE: Probably psychosomatic.

ENID: I don't think Dr. Proctor has heard of psychosomatic. He's about twice as old as I am, and for the last fifteen years he's been putting everything down to the change of life. And I always have to take my clothes off. M.D. in his case stands for Mucky Devil. However, one shouldn't complain, should one, Mr. Lowther? One's lucky to reach sixty without some darns and patches in the human fabric.

GEORGE: Are you sixty?

ENID: Sixty-two, dear. Yes, sixty-two. I'm into the home stretch now. The coda. The run up to the springboard. Time's up, come in No. 17. No, no, you want to say. Not me. *Her*. I haven't had a long enough turn. She started off ages before me. But that's where the management exercises its absolute discretion.

GEORGE: Enid, you are all right, aren't you?

ENID: 'Course I am, dear. It's just an old woman rambling on. I haven't done too badly for all that. Though occasionally the system needs a little prompting. I've made it a rule never to go far without a packet of prunes. Don't pull a face, dear. Sex and bowels, I know. Shut up, Enid. I shall end up in a Home for Insufferables in Rickmansworth.

GEORGE: Not while I'm here, you won't.

ENID: Oh, Georgie. (*Kisses him.*)

GEORGE: Another drink?

ENID: No. No. Or I shall be better company than a lady should. Better be making tracks. Home again, home again, jiggety jig.

BRIAN: I can lift you as far as Baker Street.

ENID: In a motor? How marvellous.

GEORGE: Are you sure you're all right going home at this time of night?

POLLY: It's only a quarter to eleven.

GEORGE: I thought you might be nervous.

ENID: Nervous? Of what? Rape. In Stanmore. No such luck. Anyway all sex is rape in Stanmore, they're such an unforthcoming lot. Where's my bag?

GEORGE: Good God, Enid. It weighs a ton.

ENID: I know. It's one of the things about getting older, there are more and more things one can't do without. In the old days when I was a student at the Slade I used to set off in the morning, slip a sandwich and a packet of ciggies into my skirt pocket and I was set up for the day. Nowadays if I don't have everything . . . books, Kleenex, pad, envelopes, scarf, cardigan . . . I'm miserable. And most times I never open the book, write a letter, wipe my nose or put on my cardigan. But I wouldn't be settled without it.

POLLY: Come on, Enid. Brian's waiting.

BRIAN: It's all right.

ENID: Coming, just—(*Powdering her face*)—just papering over the cracks. Do you mind if I just pop upstairs to the lavvy?

POLLY: Oh, God, that's another half-hour. Don't wake the children.

ENID: I don't really want to go but one never knows whether one's going to see another, does one.

(*Exits by stairs door.*)

BRIAN: How's Andy?

POLLY: He's doing his mock A levels next week. He's fine.

GEORGE: You see, *that's* news to me. I never even see him. The only one of the family who appears to have inherited my intellectual abilities and I never see him from one week end to the next. This is simply his campaign headquarters, he's here just long enough to get some more lead put in his pencil, then off.

POLLY: All imagination. He's not even my flesh and blood and I know him better than you do.

GEORGE: You see him occasionally, that's why.

(ENID *enters from stairs door with* GEOFF.)

ENID: I've found an unauthorized man on the landing.

POLLY: Geoff, I'd forgotten you were in the house.

GEOFF: I've measured it all up.

POLLY: Geoff's making us an airing cupboard.

GEORGE: I hope it's all right tomorrow.

ENID: Oh, yes, silly. Now, young man, let us hie hence in yon Aston Martin.

BRIAN: It's an M.G. actually.

POLLY: Geoff lives Notting Hill way. Do you want lifting? Brian, you don't know Geoff, do you?

BRIAN: How do you do. It'll be a bit of a squeeze.

ENID: Good.

(GEORGE *goes out with them carrying* ENID'*s bag.*)

ENID: George, did I ever tell you: Sickert once pinched my bottom. You could see the mark for weeks.

(POLLY *and* GEOFF *are left.* POLLY *is flustered and tired.*)

POLLY: Good night, Geoff. I still haven't got your number.

GEOFF: Haven't you? I'm not on the phone.

POLLY: I never looked out that shrapnel.

GEOFF: What?

POLLY: That shrapnel. Last week, I . . .

GEOFF: Yes, if it's not any trouble.

POLLY: No, it's not any trouble. I've been keeping my eyes open for the other, but I haven't . . .

GEOFF: I fancy you.

POLLY: Yes, I do. I mean . . . yes.

GEOFF: See you.

(POLLY *and* GEORGE *now prepare for bed.* POLLY *clearing up the house.* GEORGE *is also tidying up.* POLLY *has a transistor with her which is playing chamber music.*)

(*A recurrent theme in the play should be* GEORGE *switching off this transistor whenever he can and* POLLY *switching it back on again when she notices. She should come back in her nightdress, with transistor and do some incongruous job that suddenly strikes her, like polishing some brass ornament or touching up a picture frame with paint. She goes out eventually turning the lights off, but* GEORGE *comes back, turns one of them on, now in his pyjamas. He looks at himself in the mirror.*)

GEORGE: When does it happen? When did I turn into this? This sagging cistern, lagged with an overcoat of flesh that gets thicker and thicker every year. The skin sags, the veins break down, more and more galleries are sealed off. And you never notice. There is no pain. No warning shots. No bells ring back at base to indicate that another section of the front line has collapsed. This is the body I live with and hoist into bed each night. I heave it desperately from place to place, dump it with less and less enthusiasm on someone else's body, then lug it off again and go about my business as a representative of the people. Save me, O God, from the Car Wash and the lawn-mower on Sundays, the steak house and the Whisky a Go Go. Deliver me from leisure and salmon pink trousers. Give me the Roman virtues, O God. Dignity, sobriety. And at the last, let my heart not be whisked across London preceded by fourteen police cars, sounding their klaxons, the transfer of my liver not be discussed by trendy surgeons (who consent willingly to make up) on late night television programmes. May I die, as I have lived, just about in one piece

35

and my carcase not be scavenged as soon as the breath can more or less safely be said to have left my body. Shovel me into the dustbin, O Lord, without reducing me to offal in some sterile and gleaming knackers yard. And make me a decent man, O God.

(*He turns off the light, and for a second or two the stage is dark. During the last speech the sound of chamber music from* POLLY's *transistor can be heard.*)

(*This now ceases, as the outside door is unlocked, by* ANDY, GEORGE's *son. He is a boy of seventeen, seen only by the light of the fridge which he opens and takes out a bottle of milk. He takes it to the mirror and drinks it, staring at himself. Goes close and looks at it for a second. Puts the milk back in the fridge, and goes out by the stairs door.*)

(*Lights dim.*)

(*The same. A few months later. Sunday.*)

(GEORGE *and* ENID *are packing up some rubbish, chiefly consisting of books;* GEORGE *is clearing out his bookshelves, running his finger down the shelves and selecting volumes he doesn't want.*)

GEORGE: What time is it? I'm supposed to put the chicken in.

ENID: Shall I do it?

GEORGE: No. It's all ready. I just have to pop it in.

ENID: I hope it's free range?

GEORGE: Fat lot you care. No. It's from one of those battery farms down near the cottage. They crack on they're Free Range establishments and a few of the hens who've earned privileges for good behaviour are allowed out in front of the sheds. Meanwhile the rest are bound and gagged inside. Battery farms. Silence, low sheds and the chimney. The blueprint for the concentration camp. Odd depressions in the ground mock the trippers herding to the coast, stir memories of woods in Silesia, huts in a clearing and a sergeant being sick by a wall. Here we are, bird. Shorn of claws and beak, slung fluttering on some overhead shuttle, to be scalded, plucked and blinded and arrive at last upon our kitchen table, plump and white and comfortable with a lemon and one or two onions to give you the savour in death you never had in life. In you go at Mark 6.

ENID: Where's Polly?

GEORGE: On safari in the East End with her faithful bearer. Apparently there is this back street in Bermondsey where Chippendale chairs are being given away for a song by people who haven't the sense they were born with. Or so they've heard.

ENID: Is there time for a cup of tea?

GEORGE: I loathe Sunday. Thank God the kids are at the Zoo.

ENID: Where's the tea? It used to be in this thing.

GEORGE: Ah no, there's been a radical re-thinking of the kitchen. It's now in the tin with the picture of the royal wedding.

ENID: H'm. I remember buying one of those at the time. I don't know. Everything's catching up. These days you can hardly keep ahead of the past. This shelf is new, too. And this cupboard.

GEORGE: Yes, both erected by Geoff, the Nazarene carpenter. I wonder whether Jesus did odd carpentry jobs around people's houses? "I'm sorry, Mrs. Cohen, I shan't be in for the next forty days. No. Not really a holiday. Just coming to terms with myself really!" Now, Enid, do I want *I've Seen 'Em All*, Memoirs of the Head Commissionaire at Claridges?

ENID: No.

GEORGE: Or *The City of Nottingham Civic Handbook 1953*? "New Factories in the Green Belt make an Imposing Prospect"
Don't want that.

ENID: Doesn't it bother you, them going off together?

GEORGE: The amanuensis? No. I mean, she wants company. But I reckon he'd as soon stuff a Chesterfield. Anyway, it doesn't mean as much to them. They aren't always sniffing round for it the way we are. He said.

ENID: Here we go, dear. We always end up talking about sex. It only happens with you.

GEORGE: Anyway, I'm the one who has to mind his P's and Q's. I've had one turn already. She's only on her first leg. You would have liked Liz, the first Mrs. Oliver. A much maligned woman.

ENID: By whom?

GEORGE: Me chiefly. No homemaker she. She was a slattern, a

soft, amiable, lovable slut. We fixed up the wedding three times and she just couldn't be bothered to get up. Politically, I need hardly say, she was of the left.

(GEORGE *possibly gets a photograph of him, Liz and Andy as a child.*)

A placid and utterly unmilitant presence at every sit-in. And the house . . . or flat, as it was then, always upside down. You'd keep on finding young men from the provinces sleeping on the floor. Fabled names in the annals of the New Left. All with monosyllabic names . . . Stan, Mike, Les, Norm. As if to have two syllables in one's name were an indication of social pretension and to prove themselves of the true faith their names had to be circumcized and trimmed of surplus syllables. What was I talking about?

ENID (*still looking at books*): Forgotten, dear. Wasn't listening.

GEORGE: Liz. She was Mrs. Jellaby, I suppose, which is partly why I swopped her for one of the crab-apple jelly brigade. No offence.

ENID: I don't mind, dear. Polly's always taken more after Leonard than she does after me.

GEORGE: I don't know that it matters. Andy was brought up on baked beans and Rice Krispies. It doesn't seem to have done him any harm. He was a real battery boy.

ENID: How is he?

(GEORGE *shrugs.*)

He has grown.

GEORGE: Yes. Seventeen. He's found his feet . . . and other parts of his anatomy.

ENID: You used to be such pals.

GEORGE: We did, didn't we. Much more than I ever was with my dad. But of course our ages were much further apart.

ENID: I don't know where she gets all this baking her own bread from. Hard to find a more fervent disciple of bought cakes than me.

GEORGE: She's simply conducting a private rearguard action against the present day. No, they weren't. Good God. My father was actually younger. He was closer to me in age than I am to Andy. He seemed ancient, always. It's ludicrous. To look at

38

us, you'd think we had a marvellous going on. We have two establishments, one here and the cottage. They're run in nice conjunction. Not a plum ripens before it is forthwith translated into jam. Not an egg is laid before it is summarily drowned in waterglass. Even the hedgerows are scoured and their wild, heedless fruit thrust beneath a polite crust. Oh, no. There's nothing wasted in this house, least of all opportunity. Scarcely does a plant poke its head above the soil before it's rudely dragged forth to jostle tulips in a vase. Sewing, reaping, stewing, steeping, the larder's stocked as if any day General Paulus might invest the doorstep for a siege of indeterminate duration. The larder is lined with jams in flavours of incestuous proximity . . . melon and marrow, lemon and ginger. Nothing, nothing is wasted. Nothing is allowed to break out of the endless cycle of retrenchment and regeneration. That cigarette end you have discarded, Vicar, it will find its way on to the compost heap. Part once more of the continuing process. Did you leave an old razor blade in the bathroom, madam? No. Don't apologize. It will go towards a bus destined for Addis Ababa.

ENID: There is something wrong, I suppose if we have to be dragged into the future. We ought to go forward with firm jaw and clear brow, all in profile like a Soviet poster. Instead of looking back, dragged behind those awful hard-faced men in the Business Supplement.

GEORGE: I wish sometimes we could just go out and buy something when we need it, without all this performance of consumers guide and best buy. I tell you. We bought that gas oven last year. There was that much consultation and consideration we might have been getting a divorce. Your house, you see, Enid, isn't like this. This isn't a house. It's a setting we've devised for ourselves. We're trying to get something over, though God knows what it is. Think of your house . . . your kitchen . . . that foxed and fly-spotted fridge on legs, your old Belling gas oven. Wood tops, stripped white and ridged by scrubbing and use rather than two days in a bath of caustic at the back of the Fulham Road. Use, not looks. Old sossed-down chairs, a house that's grown out of the life lived there, not a setting in which that life is lived.

ENID: You are an old snob, George. More right wing every day. What you want is an old-fashioned middle-class household.

GEORGE: That's not right wing. But I do. The middle-class family . . . the most exclusive interior decorator in the world. An old brown carpet slipper of a house, comfortable, roomy and lived in. This . . . this is scenery. It's been dropped in from the flies.

ENID: It'll age. It'll mellow.

GEORGE: The nicest part of your house, the thing that stamps it straightaway, so that you know exactly where you are, what level of society you're moving at, is the vestibule. That bit between the front and the inside door. Plants, a pot containing various of Leonard's broken walking-sticks. A croquet mallet and an old lacrosse stick, and a disgusting raincoat. I know that that particular sort of shabby gentility will always elude us. Our house will never look like that if we live till we're ninety-five. Better the past a void than survive like this. We're accomplices, Polly and me, with snake-hipped young men totting up back lanes in Grimthorpe and Featherstone, knocking on doors in Bishop Auckland, peering in through barricades of plants and ornaments for miners' widows gone a bit silly and willing to trade the polished artefacts of a life's history for a few quid. Reft of their associations, stripped like the eternal pine of the polish of memory and affection and association and brought back from northern counties to this sly southern air across the saddle bow of some chiffon-scarved Genghis Khan with a shop down Camden Passage and an eye for the coming thing. You're quiet.

ENID (laughs): Good job one of us is. I'm all right.

GEORGE: Have you been feeling any better?

ENID: Oh, yes. Yes. Heaps.

GEORGE: Don't want you. Nor you. (Chucking books in the box.) (He stands back and looks at the bookshelf.)
It's still no different. All those greens and yellows and blues. It looks like a caravan site in book form.

ENID: Oh, no, love. They're very cheerful. I like a bright bookcase.

GEORGE: There again. Why don't my bookshelves look like my

tutor's did . . . faded crumbling browns, sun-bleached dust-wrapper.

ENID: It's what's in them that counts.

GEORGE: They've got no dignity. They're on the game. Tarts for some smart publishing ponce. "Hello, dearie, don't you recognize me in my new yellow plastic? It's Jane Austen, dear, in my new uniform edition. Do you like it? We've had some times together, haven't we? You've taken me to bed more times than I care to remember." Look out. They're here.

(GEORGE *and* ENID *now sit silent as* POLLY *and* GEOFF *slowly edge into the room.*)

POLLY: Just wait till you see this!

GEOFF: It's the most incredible thing, George, it really is. Look at that!

GEORGE: But it's a tombstone.

POLLY: Well, it was. It isn't now.

ENID: It's going to take some cleaning.

GEOFF: I'll give it a wash.

ENID: Where did it come from?

GEOFF: Fell off the back of a churchyard.

GEORGE: "Sacred to the memory of Joseph Banks, who departed this life August 16, 1842. Aged 28 years."

POLLY: How's the chicken?

GEORGE: It won't be done yet.

POLLY: I'd better get my skates on.

GEORGE: Did Brian say he was coming?

POLLY: He wasn't sure. Give him a ring. Leonard and the children are staying at the zoo, aren't they? Enid, come and help me lay the table.

(GEORGE *dials.*)

ENID: Oh, yes, sorry, dear.

GEORGE: Lines to Manchester are engaged. Please try again later. I'm not ringing Manchester.

ENID: I shouldn't fancy it. What are you going to do with it?

POLLY: No need to do anything with it. It's something in its own right.

GEOFF: I'm going to make it into a coffee table.

41

GEORGE: And what about him?

POLLY: Who?

GEORGE: Joseph Banks, now lying in some nameless grave, patiently awaiting the Resurrection. Well, this is it, Joseph. Everlasting life as a coffee table in Highgate. Enid, do you fancy a walk on to the end to get some beer?

ENID: Lovely. Hold on while I just gild the lily. Then we'll pop along to the local.

GEORGE: No. Not the local. It's just the nearest pub. It's only the local if you subscribe to some nice consoling myth of community life.

POLLY: And don't stop there boozing. This won't be long. And where are you taking all those?

(GEORGE *is carrying out the carton of books.*)

GEORGE: These, my dear, are going to their long home.

POLLY: Oh, George, they might come in handy for . . .

GEORGE: No. They would not come in handy for anything. They are not going to Oxfam; they are not going to the Thrift Shop. They are going into the dustbin where they belong.

POLLY: Perhaps Geoff could use them.

GEORGE: No. Nobody can use them. Nobody is going to use them. They are rubbish, waste, junk. (*He is triumphant.*) DUST-BIN HO!

(GEORGE *and* ENID *depart and we hear the clank of a dustbin lid.* POLLY *comes over to* GEOFF. *They hold each other,* GEOFF *with his back to the audience staring over her shoulder at the book-case.*)

GEOFF: Has he read all these?

(*He picks out a book, without disengaging* POLLY.)

POLLY: Doubt it. That's mine. Empson. *Seven Types of Ambiguity.* I actually made notes on it.

GEOFF: Would I like that?

POLLY (*almost laughing*): No. (*Then seeing the offence.*) No.

GEOFF: I might.

POLLY: You wouldn't.

GEOFF: You mean, I wouldn't understand it.

POLLY: No. I mean, yes. But I shouldn't bother. Most of these are a waste of time.

42

GEOFF: Is it non-fiction?

POLLY: Yes. (*Again laughing and upsetting him.*)

GEOFF: Is it I'm not fit to read them or they're too hard for me to read?

POLLY: They wouldn't interest you. Geoff. Read what you like. Don't go into a huff. What does it matter, anyway? It's all going to be cassettes now, isn't it?

(*Sound of someone coming in and they break up.* BRIAN *enters with a couple of bottles of wine.* GEOFF *kneels at the gravestone, cleaning it.*)

BRIAN: Here I am with my little lot. Am I welcome or am I not?

(*He raises his hand in greeting to* GEOFF, *sees the stone and begins to advance on it.*)

POLLY (*quickly*): Come and give me a hand with the lunch.

BRIAN: Yes. Yes. Yes. Yes.

(BRIAN *winks at* GEOFF.)

You making yourself useful?

GEOFF: You bet.

BRIAN: Friend of yours? What's the matter?

(BRIAN *walks round it, without saying anything, then steps over it.*)

Somebody walked over your grave? Ho ho.

(*He touches* GEOFF *with his shoe.*)

GEOFF (*in an undertone*): Knock it off, will you?

POLLY: George is a bore. He's just thrown away a whole jorum of stuff. They'd have made such a lovely parcel for Oxfam. Geoff, nip out and see whether he's chucked out anything worth keeping. I can't bear it. You can have whatever you want.

BRIAN: Do you think Oxfam ever return anything? Oxfam graciously acknowledges the receipt of your gift but feel they must return this pair of old knickers as they would only aggravate the situation. How many are we? (*As he lays the table.*)

POLLY: Five. I don't think Andy's in. Give him a shout.

(BRIAN *shouts upstairs.*)

BRIAN: Andy! No.

(POLLY *scatters potato peelings on the floor.*)

43

POLLY: Oh, Dame Agnes, if you could see me now.
(*She still has hold of the book* GEOFF *picked out and is looking at her notes.*)

BRIAN: Dame Agnes who?

POLLY: Dame Agnes Bemrose, Mistress of Girton, the apple of whose eye I for a short time was.

BRIAN: Are we having a pudding?

POLLY: No-o. She thought I had a great future.

BRIAN: As what?

POLLY: It was never specified. I once fancied I'd like to be Mistress of Girton, then I decided I'd settle for being a lady novelist, rather along the lines of Virginia Woolf, and then that, too, dwindled into getting into the BBC. And now here I am, ankle deep in blighted hopes and potato peelings. "Remember, Miss Baker, there is no Nobel Prize for Knitting."

BRIAN: I never thought of you as at all academic. You're not that sort at all. Like me.

POLLY: Did you never want to go to university?

BRIAN: Didn't mind. Could have done. Went straight into the works instead. I wanted to get started.

POLLY: I was a bright girl. I had some interesting ideas on Coleridge's inner landscape. Then George came down to speak to the Labour Club one night in the Spring Term and that was it. You'd have done very well.

BRIAN: Not then. Now perhaps. I liked provincial life. The works all week, rugger with the boys on Saturdays and a piss-up in Knutsford afterwards. I reckon it was the army changed me. But for a certain medical corporal I was all headed for a smart wedding at the cathedral and two pages of photographs in *Cheshire Life*, winter holidays in the Bahamas and two piggy children at Oundle.

POLLY: Education didn't alter me one bit. Falling in love, sex, the children, they've altered me. I had a good education but it never went to my head, somehow. It should be a journey ending up with you at a different place. It didn't take with me. My degree was a kind of inoculation. I got just enough education to make me immune to it for the rest of my life. Now I

44

couldn't tell you the first thing about Coleridge's inner land-scape. All wasted.

BRIAN: I don't want to know about Coleridge, thank you. I just want my lunch. Or dinner as my father the millowner would say.

POLLY: Anyway, it's a good thing I didn't get a better degree or George would never have married me.

BRIAN: Come on.

POLLY: True. That's why he got rid of the first Mrs. Oliver. She was too clever by half. But I haven't changed. Coleridge's imagery. Odd bits of junk. Picking up bits of stuff other people haven't spotted. What medical corporal?

BRIAN: Never mind.

POLLY: Now Andy's talking about leaving school, doing something useful. I haven't dared tell George. What does it matter. It doesn't get you any further, education.

BRIAN: It's not designed to. Or rather it is designed to, and that's what's wrong with it. Or so George would say. We in the Conservative Party think exactly the opposite.

POLLY: I don't know what you think at all. You don't care much, do you?

BRIAN: Not much, no.

POLLY: And Parliament. That either?

BRIAN: Passes the time. Fills in that awkward gap between the cradle and the grave.

(BRIAN *sees the postcard he gave* POLLY *stuck in the mirror. He viciously takes it out, and tears it up.*)

POLLY: Brian, I liked that.

BRIAN: Here's another one instead.

(*Takes out another postcard.*)

POLLY: Is it the same one?

BRIAN: I expect so.

POLLY: No message. Do you get lots of them?

BRIAN: Not lots. Every three months maybe.

POLLY: But why? It must be somebody who's mad.

BRIAN: Not entirely. I always get one if I've been in the news, or on television. If I raise my voice anywhere.

POLLY: What for, if there's no message? It's not even like an anonymous letter.

BRIAN: Oh, but there is a message, you see. He knows what it means and I know what it means.

POLLY: What?

BRIAN: A long time ago, at least, not so long really, when I'd just come out of the army and was still full time at the works. Before I was an M.P. Quite a long time before, in fact, he must have been very smart to pick it out I was the same person.

POLLY: What same person?

BRIAN: I was had up for you know what with some youth in Victoria Park, Oswestry.

POLLY: I never knew that.

BRIAN: I should hope not. Mind you, it was so dull. It wasn't even in the papers. But *he* knows, whoever he is.

POLLY: How foul. Why don't you go to the police?

BRIAN: What for? It's not blackmail. It's just a picture of Victoria Park, Oswestry. It's actually a new one, that one. I haven't had that one before. The other one used to be rather a nice sepia photograph. They've obviously run out of stock.

POLLY: Well, I'm not having it up there. (*She tears it up.*) Why did you never say?

BRIAN: It's funny the place, really, isn't it? Lavatories, public parks, cinemas in the afternoon, the places where it happens. It can't ever be tragic, sad even, the setting's so banal. Nothing to say, why should I? Every now and again somebody pops down the road to the post. I've got now so that I can almost feel them coming.

POLLY: People are foul.

BRIAN: Yours, A Well-wisher.

(GEOFF *comes back, and* POLLY *starts to bustle round again.*)

GEOFF: What a load of old rubbish!

BRIAN: So why all this fuss about James. If it didn't take with you, why bother?

POLLY: He's a boy. He's got to get on in the world. He can't rely on being seduced at the Labour Club dance.

BRIAN: He could always try the Conservative Club.

POLLY: Watch it, you'll corrupt the youth.

46

(GEOFF *is still cleaning the gravestone.*)

BRIAN: Youth? Servants. (*He taps* GEOFF *with his foot.*)

POLLY: Geoff isn't servants, are you, love?

GEOFF: Aren't I?

POLLY: No, course you're not.

GEOFF: No, say it. Servants. Yes. We're servants for the people
who aren't used to having servants, servants who don't make
you feel guilty about it. That's probably because you're not
sure our lives aren't better than yours.

POLLY: Look, Geoff, I said I was sorry.

GEOFF: Skip it.

(GEORGE *enters breathless.*)

GEORGE: Where's the bucket?

POLLY: What bucket?

GEORGE: The bucket. Quick, quick, for God's sake, where's the
bucket?

POLLY: What bucket?

GEORGE: The *bucket*. The bowl, anything. Come *on*. It's the dog.
It's there.

POLLY: What? Oh, no, George, you can't.

GEORGE: Yes, I bloody well can.

(*He rushes out with the dripping pail. Shouts outside as he
throws the water. He returns, satisfied.*)

Got it. Purple in the face as it was passing some particularly
recalcitrant stool. It leaped out of its skin. Sodden.

POLLY: It's not the dog's fault.

GEORGE: Maybe. Sometimes I think St. Francis of Assisi was bark-
ing up the wrong tree. Of course it's the dog's fault. If it will
choose our step.

(*He is about to throw another one, when there is a knocking at
the door.* GEORGE *opens it, bucket in hand, sees who it is, turns
round smartly and comes away from the door, followed in by* MRS.
BRODRIBB.)

MRS BRODRIBB: One moment, young man. Some person on these
premises has just thrown a bucket of water over my dog. I
have just met him running down the street soaked to the skin.

GEORGE: Your dog, Mrs. Brodribb?

MRS. BRODRIBB: My dog, Mr. Oliver.

47

POLLY: What makes you think it was here?

GEORGE: Polly. If by dog, Mrs Brodribb, you mean that polka-dotted sewage machine on legs, yes. It was me.

MRS. BRODRIBB: So, you admit it . . . he admits it. You ought to be ashamed of yourself, a man in your position, an unprovoked assault.

GEORGE: Unprovoked? Unprovoked? Mrs. Brodribb, I have lost count of the number of times that creature has fouled our doorstep. It's every time he shoves his arse outside your door.

MRS. BRODRIBB: Arse! Oh!

POLLY: It does happen rather often, Mrs. Brodribb. I'm sure my husband didn't mean to harm him, only to teach him a lesson.

MRS. BRODRIBB: If you wanted to attack a defenceless dog why didn't you choose one your own size? They have to go some-where.

GEORGE: Then why not on your own doorstep then?

MRS. BRODRIBB: Because he needs the walk. Besides, you should be flattered.

POLLY: Flattered!

MRS. BRODRIBB: When Max . . .

GEOFF: Max!

MRS. BRODRIBB (*silencing him with a look*): . . . pauses by your door-step he is not simply relieving himself. He is leaving a mes-sage, a sign, a note.

GEORGE: A message, is it? Then I wish he wasn't quite such a frequent correspondent. Your dog, Mrs. Brodribb, is a proper little Mme de Sévigné. Besides, who is it leaving a message for, for God's sake? Not for anybody at this address. We haven't any dogs. We have a goldfish and a hamster. Surely he's not contemplating starting up a deviant relationship with them?

MRS. BRODRIBB: Don't you be sarcastic with me. I don't want any of your House of Commons manners here. I know one thing. I shan't ever vote Socialist after this. Not that I ever did.

GEORGE: And another thing, Mrs. Brodribb. This leaving notes business. Presumably it's to do with . . . I'm sorry to have to mention this word . . . but it has to do with sex, hasn't it?

MRS. BRODRIBB (*who has been circling round the company, stares long and deep into BRIAN's face*): I've seen you on television, too.

You're all the same.

GEORGE: Sex, Mrs. Brodribb. But Max can go on leaving little notes for other dogs on our step until he's blue in the face, but I bet you never let him out to back them up, do you? Except once a year with some other equally spotted bitch under medical supervision at forty guineas a time in some foul kennels in Hounslow. So what's all this message leaving, Mrs. Brodribb? What are all these notes? I'll tell you what Max is, Mrs. Brodribb. He's all talk and no trousers. But for future reference I am not going to have my doorstep used as a post-restante by frustrated dalmatians who never come. And I mean come, Mrs. Brodribb.

POLLY: We have got a bit fed up of it.

MRS. BRODRIBB: It? It? What you call it, Mrs. Oliver, is an extremely sensitive creature, twice champion in his class at Crufts and a thoroughbred dalmatian. That dog, as you call it, has ten times more breeding than you have.

GEORGE: Mrs. Brodribb. Shit has no pedigree.

MRS. BRODRIBB: Did you hear that? Did you hear that? Such . . . language, and from one of our elected representatives. But I give you fair warning, if there is any repetition of this incident, if you ever interfere with Max again, I shall be forced to fetch my husband, diabetic though he be. And that's my last word.

GEOFF: Aw, piss off, you old cow.

(ENID *comes in with a jug just as* MRS. BRODRIBB *is going out.*)

MRS. BRODRIBB: If we had a real Conservative government I should have you horsewhipped.

(ENID *is mystified,* GEOFF *bursts out laughing, and there is a general hubbub.*)

(ENID *goes upstage into the kitchen with* GEORGE *and* BRIAN *and is told about* MRS. BRODRIBB *in half-heard dialogue which goes on under the action, from various people.*)

ALL: She's a silly woman from the other end of the road. George just threw a bucket of water over her dog. The dalmatian. Ought to have thrown it over her. Quite. Who wants beer? How many are we? I hope the chicken'll be big enough. Where's salt and pepper, etc. etc?

(POLLY *comes downstage where* GEOFF *is still fiddling with the tombstone.*)

POLLY: Come on, Geoff.

GEOFF: In a sec.

(ANDY *comes in by the outside door.*)

GEORGE: Now. I never forget a face. That, unless I'm very much mistaken, is my son.

ANDY: There you go, George. Go to the top of the class.

POLLY: Andy!

ENID: Come, give me a kiss, dear. Mmm. Isn't his hair lovely. Lovely. Mmm.

POLLY: Wash your hands, love, we're all ready.

ENID: How lovely. Where've you been, dear?

ANDY: Been over the park.

BRIAN: Does it matter where we all sit?

(POLLY *indicating places.*)

POLLY: George, Enid, Andy, me, Brian.

ENID: How lovely, we're all together.

POLLY: And Geoff.

(GEOFF *comes slowly to the table as the curtain comes down.*)

END OF ACT ONE

ACT TWO

GEORGE *and* POLLY *are getting ready to go out.* GEOFF *is busy putting yet more shelves up in the kitchen.* POLLY *is ironing her skirt for the function, or sewing something onto her dress.* GEORGE *is in a dress shirt. It is evening and the children, as ever, are in bed.*

GEORGE: Put my cuff-links in, will you?

POLLY: Geoff'll do it. I've still got to get washed.

    (GEORGE *goes over to* GEOFF.)

GEORGE (*to* POLLY): You're going to have to get a move on. (*To* GEOFF.) Are you baby-sitting?

GEOFF: Me? No. You're dropping me off, aren't you? (*To* POLLY.)

POLLY: Andy's sitting. I asked him this morning.

GEORGE (*edging over to the table where his watch is, so that* GEOFF *has to follow him still trying to put in his links*): Does he know what time we've got to be there?

POLLY: Don't get all agitato.

GEORGE: What time have we got to be there? Thank you.

GEOFF (*looking at card in mirror*): Eight.

POLLY: Eight for anything or just eight?

GEOFF: Eight.

POLLY: That means eight-fifteen.

GEORGE: It means eight. It isn't as if we were just going out to Enid or somebody.

POLLY: Better start ringing a taxi.

GEORGE: The car should have been back today.

POLLY: I don't know why we bother with the garage. Geoff is marvellous with engines.

GEORGE (*telephoning*): There ought to be somewhere to go to get not only service for the car but also absolution for the sin of

51

owning it.

POLLY: Sin. I don't know what we'd do without it.

GEORGE: What I would like is the bare essentials, a car like a monastic cell swept clean of dangling dolls, jokey notices, scatter cushions and . . . Hello. I want a taxi, please, to . . . Ah you're not 3232. I did dial it. Sorry you've been troubled. Good-bye, madam. A car shot of all the paraphernalia of dedicated motoring. What I want is an Austin Ascetic, a Morris Monk or a Triumph Trappist. Good evening. Could we have a taxi, please, in about . . . how long?

POLLY: Three-quarters of an hour.

GEORGE: Half an hour; 17 Passfield Gardens, Highgate. The name is Oliver.

POLLY: Say M.P. It always helps.

GEORGE: M.P. I wasn't giving you my initials. Never mind. The number is Dickens 0310. Dickens of *Oliver Twist* fame. DIC is the *same* as the code. I know the post office is asking us to use all figure numbers. But I am ringing up for a taxi not for the latest developments in telecommunications.

POLLY: We'll never get one if you're rude to them. For God's sake, be NICE.

GEORGE: The Dickens number is 432 . . . I mean 342 . . . 0310. Yes, I will hold on. Geoff, hold on for me, will you?

POLLY: I wish it wasn't tonight. We shall miss you on the telly.

GEORGE: It's old stock most of it. (*Picking up some ornament.*) Where's this thing from?

POLLY: It's a present.

GEORGE: Who the hell from?

POLLY: . . . from Geoff.

GEORGE: Oh, sorry.

(POLLY *winks at* GEOFF *behind* GEORGE's *back.* GEORGE *does his shirt up in front of the mirror and puts on his tie—he has cut himself shaving.*)

POLLY: Watch the iron for me, love, will you.

(GEOFF, *with the receiver to his ear, is now watching the iron also.*)

GEORGE: I think I've broken off my tooth again. (*He examines his mouth in the mirror.*) My mouth is beginning to look like the

52

ruins of Hamburg.

POLLY: I can't understand you having such bad teeth. Mine are
perfect.

GEOFF: It's through not having oranges in the war.

POLLY: Why is it only teeth that decay?

GEORGE: It isn't.

POLLY: You don't always have to go to the doctors to have holes
in your arms stopped up, do you? Or your legs filled. It's a
flaw in the design.

GEORGE: That's one thing I envy . . . no resent . . . in Andy. For
all the fact he was brought up on an exclusive diet of baked
beans and liquorice allsorts he has perfectly even teeth.
Whereas mine are as yellow and pitted as a pub lavatory. I
open my mouth and there's so much gold it's like a glimpse
of the vaults at Fort Knox.

GEOFF: Hold on. (*Hands receiver to* GEORGE.)

GEORGE: Yes. Yes. What? Nearer the time. (*To* POLLY.) They want
us to ring nearer the time.

POLLY: But it is nearer the time.

GEORGE (*to receiver*): But it is nearer the time. Nearer still. You're
sure there'll be one? Yes, yes. Good-bye.

(*The children start making a din upstairs.*)

(GEORGE *goes to the stairs door and half-way up the stairs.*)

GEORGE: James. You shouldn't be out of bed. Go back to bed.
What? What does she say, James? No, she can't have her
pram in bed. She's brushed her teeth.

POLLY: Oh, yes, she can.

GEORGE: James. You can tell Elizabeth that decision has now been
countermanded on higher authority. She can have her pram
in bed. Oh God. Trouble with children . . . they're so child-
ish. If only they were older.

POLLY: They'll get older . . . in time.

(POLLY *takes off her blouse and puts on the one she's been ironing.*)

Be a love, Geoff, and tell them a story.

(GEOFF *goes upstairs.*)

GEORGE: You ought to be a bit more careful, undressing in front
of Geoff. You embarrass him.

POLLY: He doesn't mind.

GEORGE: He'll think you're doing it on purpose.

POLLY: You said it embarrasses him. You mean it embarrasses you. You forget I was brought up a member of the middle classes. We are not embarrassed by our bodies.

GEORGE: You are thirty-two. You are rapidly approaching the age when your body, whether it embarrasses you or not, begins to embarrass other people.

POLLY: Speak for yourself.

GEORGE: I do not fart about the house in my underpants.

POLLY: I've seen you in your underpants.

GEORGE: Of course you've seen me in my underpants. You are my wife. Seeing me in my underpants is part of the duties, responsibilities and possibly even the pleasures of marriage. All I am saying is that I do not fart about in the house in them. You have never seen me in this room, for instance, in my underpants.

(POLLY *thinks very hard.*)

POLLY (*triumphantly*): Yes, I have.

GEORGE: When?

(POLLY *crestfallen. She can't remember.*)

We ought to be making tracks.

POLLY: No. I know I have.

GEORGE: I'm sorry we're late, Prime Minister, but my wife and I were detained in argument, as to when was the last occasion she saw me in the living-room in my underpants.

POLLY: And saying that about his present.

GEORGE: I didn't know it was his. Be honest, you don't like it . . .

POLLY: No, but, I'm trying to encourage him. Educate him a bit.

GEORGE: What in? The liberal art of accumulating unwanted scrap. I suppose you think by teaching him to line his nice little Notting Hill nest with articles like that is education.

POLLY: It's a kind of education. It's better than nothing.

GEORGE: It's corruption. He'd be better off with the usual fifteen Penguins and a blow-up of Buster Keaton.

(GEORGE *is by now more or less kitted out. He puts on his jacket and regards himself in the mirror.*)

I wish I was a bit more left wing. Then I needn't wear this

54

thing on grounds of conscience.

POLLY: You look very good. Really slim.

(*Pause.*)

You aren't going in those socks?

GEORGE: What socks? I haven't got any others.

POLLY: You can't go to Downing Street in grey socks. What if somebody looks up your legs?

GEORGE: As I'm swinging from the chandelier, you mean? If one remembers that the Lord Chancellor wears button boots and football socks, I reckon these are pretty discreet.

POLLY: I wonder what colour Geoff's socks are?

(*She makes for the stairs door.*)

GEORGE: I am not wearing Geoff's socks.

POLLY: Here. I know.

(*She goes to a drawer and takes out a pair of worn black tights.*)

I knew these would come in.

(*She starts cutting off the legs about half-way up.*)

GEORGE: I can't wear those. They're yours. They won't fit me.

POLLY: They stretch, stupid.

GEORGE: Anyway, they're very hot to the feet. I shall sweat.

POLLY: You're a Socialist. They expect you to sweat.

GEORGE: "I wonder whether you'd be interested to know, Prime Minister, that beneath this suave Geraldo-like exterior, I am wearing a pair of ladies' black tights." "Really? This is something that transcends politics. Tell me more." I'll feel easier when Andy turns up.

POLLY: He's generally very reliable.

GEORGE: Probably servicing some sixteen-year-old classmate with more abortions than O levels.

(GEORGE *picks up the telephone to ring a taxi again.*)

He's on the phone. Andy, where are you? We're stuck here waiting to go out. You're supposed to be at home babysitting. What? . . . (*To* POLLY.) He is at home. He's upstairs. Sorry. No, no. Carry on. Be my guest. I'm only the subscriber.

(*He puts the receiver down, then picks it up again, and listens.*)

POLLY: George!

GEORGE: Ssh! (*After a while putting it down.*) They weren't even talking about me.

POLLY: Why should they be?

GEORGE: I am just curious to know what he is like when I'm not there, that's all. Anyway, I am ready. (*He settles down on the sofa.*) Time for a few apoplectic moments with the *Daily Express*.

POLLY: Try that taxi again.

GEORGE: Give it five minutes. Here we are. "Pru Venables, niece of Rear-Admiral Sir Murdo Venables. Pru . . . here seen showing a larger expanse of upper thigh than her work with mentally handicapped children would seem to warrant, though, you will note, with her parts discreetly veiled in shadow, thinks Mr. Heath is super."
(*He gets the scissors and cuts it out and sticks it with the other cuttings on the wall.*)

POLLY: How's Brian. Did you have lunch yesterday?

GEORGE: I had lunch with him yesterday. Aren't you getting ready?

POLLY: What about?

GEORGE: Just lunch.

POLLY: No more postcards?

GEORGE: Postcards? He didn't say. Forget about it. It's not so extraordinary really. Somebody who's mad. If you ever raise your voice in public you know damn well before you've got two words out there'll be some clown stampeding for the Basildon Bond. "Any Answers", that's the real voice of the English people. Envious, cruel, angry and complacent. And the *Express*. It's nice to know the enemy's still there.
(ANDY *appears.*)
What-ho. By salad cream out of fish fingers, my Birds Eye boy.

ANDY: Light my fire. Is there any food?
(ANDY *kisses* POLLY. *And dashes dandruff off* GEORGE's *shoulders.*)

GEORGE: Sorry. It must have come off the comb.

ANDY: There you go, George. Smart.

GEORGE: I don't often wear it, it's . . .

ANDY: No. No. It suits you.

POLLY: Doesn't it?

ANDY: It's you, Dad. Very fetching. Quite the Young Conservative.

56

GEORGE: What's happening about school, said he, shifting smartly to the offensive.

POLLY: Not now, George, there isn't time.

GEORGE: You're the one who hasn't got any time. Jillo. Come on. Put your skates on. Have you thought what you want to do yet? I mean, eventually.

ANDY: No.

GEORGE: No.

(*Pause.*)

Nothing at all?

ANDY: I'd sort of hoped, you know, I was going to want to become an architect.

GEORGE: Yes.

ANDY: But it doesn't seem to be coming, the urge, so now I think I ought to drift for a bit.

(GEORGE *is silent.*)

I'm easy . . . I . . . you know . . . I . . . don't care.

GEORGE: I know you don't care. . . . What I don't see is why you have to care.

ANDY: But look, then say I don't care. Which I don't . . .

GEORGE: Andy, care about what?

ANDY: About the work, you know, what I'm doing, I, you know, well, I go along with it, right. I get my A levels, say. I don't care. I get a degree, maybe say . . . I don't care. I get a job. I don't care. I mean, George. When does it happen? When do I start to come into it? Me. Not until I've got this sodding great jingling ring of qualifications to unlock the doors I'm not particular to go into. So why not stuff it right now? I was trying to see the point of it. And that if I went to university it would be a waste of time. It's three years of my life.

(*Here or elsewhere* POLLY *should interrupt scene, without speaking, by rushing in looking for things, e.g. toilet roll, or searching in cupboards, finding what she wants and going out again.*)

GEORGE: Three years! Look, how old are you? Eighteen.

ANDY: Seventeen.

GEORGE: Seventeen. I didn't even get to university till I was twenty-two. I was stuck on some deserted aerodrome in the

57

twilight of Empire for two years first. You'll be finished when you're twenty-two. And you talk about time. Time is the one thing you have got. If there's one thing I envy you for, it's not your cool and your easy birds and an arse like a split grapefruit, it's time. You've got all the time in the world. You've still got the option. And this time, the drifting, what will you do with it, now that you've got it?

ANDY: Travel, social work. I hadn't thought.

GEORGE: No, I seem to be the only one doing any thinking. What sort of social work?

ANDY: Stop trying to pin me down.

GEORGE: All work is social work if you do it right.

ANDY: He said.

GEORGE: And if society's organized right.

ANDY: But it isn't, is it? You can't see it, because you're involved in the system.

GEORGE: System. The phrases are so worn I wonder you've the face to use them. System. What system? The system that makes me thirty years older than you are. The system of me not being willing, or indeed able to pour myself into a pair of turquoise matador pants and grow ringlets down to my shoulders. The system of clinging to plain hard logical thought instead of being at the whim of vague gusts of feeling and fellowship. Yes, I am part of that system.

ANDY: No. It's, like, sharing. You know. Being kind to one an-other. The system feeds you palliatives. The whole meaning of life is lost.

GEORGE: So. What does it mean? You say we're losing it—you must know what it is.

ANDY: It's not saying that's mine, that's yours. Not caring about colour, race . . .

GEORGE: Do I care about colour?

ANDY: I didn't say you did.

GEORGE: Well then . . .

(POLLY *comes in and out quickly.*)

POLLY: Have you got that taxi?

(GEORGE *goes on with his conversation with* ANDY *as he tele-phones.*)

58

ANDY: You see, George, you've only got to read Marx to see . . .

GEORGE: I have only to . . . No. *You* have only got to read Marx. I already have. What do you think I was doing stuck on my bed in the R.A.F. for two years? Anyway, where've you been doing Marx?

ANDY: We do it in Religious Instruction.

GEORGE: Ah.

ANDY: Dave says . . .

GEORGE: *Who* says?

ANDY: Dave. He's taking us for teaching practice.

GEORGE: Dave. Dave.

ANDY: He says . . .

GEORGE: There's no need to tell me what Dave says. I know what the Daves of this world say.

ANDY: But you don't, George. You never listen. It's just your disillusion. You lump people together, goodies and baddies. You don't differentiate between . . .

(GEORGE *holds up his hand to stop him*.)

GEORGE: Hallo. I want a taxi to 17 Passfield Gardens, Highgate. Yes . . . yes, I did ring before if you remem . . . My number is Dick . . . sorry 342 0310. Yes . . . yes . . . I'll hold on. . . . Love is all you need. That's your philosophy, isn't it? Come to me at forty trailing your wife and kids and your whole communal family when any number of joints won't disguise the fact you're fat and cross and tired and tell me then that love is all you need. Try getting that together. Yes . . . yes . . . Passfield Gardens.

ANDY: George. I have said, you know, nothing.

GEORGE: That's "you know" right. You have said "you know" bugger all. Love is not all you need.

ANDY: I never said it was.

GEORGE: No. That's how subtle you are. But you bloody well think it.

ANDY: I've said nothing. I've made no charges. What I think you don't know. You've not the faintest idea. You're not even interested. It's shadow boxing.

GEORGE: Knowledge and subtlety and understanding and law. . . . I am holding on, madam, like grim death . . . law, that's what

59

you need. Grubbing away on committees and nagging at officials and teasing away at the law; taking it in and letting it out until it fits even approximately the people who have to wear it.

ANDY: And talk, George. You forget talk. Lots and lots of talk. Witty talk. Clever talk. Dirty talk. Parliamentary talk. You're a killer, Dad, you really are.

GEORGE: Listen. Shocking though it may seem to your mawkish Maoist mentality ninety per cent of the people in this world are thick. Stupid.

ANDY: Who, Dad? You, me? Not you, me. The others.

GEORGE: That's right. The others. People who with pushing and planning, welfare and incentives can just about be brought to see their own nose end . . . And by that nose end they are led. By me. And in due course by you.

ANDY: You're wrong, George. You are wrong. Look, each person is special . . .

GEORGE: Special. On the Kingston By-Pass on a Sunday afternoon show me how special.

ANDY: Not if you like them . . . if you try and . . .

GEORGE: Liking them doesn't feed them, and liking doesn't house them. Liking them doesn't stop them turning the place into a midden or turning out in their stinking, fuming tin boxes. Sunday by Sunday perambulating their boredom about the countryside.

(*Pause.*)

So what are you going to do?

ANDY: I've told you. I don't know.

GEORGE: Of course you could go into Oxfam, or War on Want. The amount of stuff we contribute they're practically family firms. I don't know, Andy. The only thing that matters in life is work. W-O-R-K.

ANDY: Come on.

GEORGE: No.

ANDY: Look, I *believe* you . . .

GEORGE: No, really. I tell you there are times when family and kids are . . . yes, I am holding . . . all the things that are supposed to make life worth living are marginal and nothing compared with work.

ANDY: But . . .

GEORGE: No, wait.

ANDY: Work. You talk about work. Parliament? You? You never stop sounding off about it . . . threatening to go back to Oxford . . .

GEORGE: I know, I know . . .

ANDY: The worst thing you ever did, you said, what dregs there are in it. Come on. I reckon it's pretty irrelevant nowadays. Esso, I.C.I., Shell. That's where the power is. The Conglomerates.

GEORGE: The what?

ANDY: The Conglomerates . . . Esso, I.C.I. . . . . Shell . . .

GEORGE: The Conglomerates. I bet that's Dave!

ANDY: Well, what did parliament ever do? It never did much for me, anyway.

GEORGE: It never did much for you . . . it brought you into the bloody world. You were born in 1953 in Charing Cross Hospital under the auspices of the National Health Service. The National Health Service, a phrase still capable of bringing a sly smile to people's faces. You shrug it off, the Welfare State, another sneering phrase. It's nothing to you. You've grown up with it, you were born under it. You take it for granted now. You don't remember the years when it was put together, at the desks of little men with bad teeth and terrible haircuts, runtish little Civil Servants born during the Depression, smoking too much in their cold government green offices in Nissen huts on bomb sites shivering through that winter of 1947 that went on until June. Hammering it out clause by clause, section by irrelevant section. Food rationed, clothes rationed, coal rationed, working by candlelight in power cuts, left standing in the Tube by the hour together. Battering it out and forcing it through in the teeth of the Conservative Party, in the teeth of the medical profession, in the rotten nicotine-stained teeth of half the nation, they got it through and laid the corner-stone of a civilized life. And I glory in that. Snobbish, sceptical sneering socialist that I am, I glory in it.

61

ANDY: Great days, Dad. Those were the days, Dad.

GEORGE: Socialist that I am I glory in it. And it was done, please note, not by kindness and benevolence, not by moist good fellowship and rattling beads and tuning into the universe. But by grit and thought and work. Back-breaking, life-destroying, ill-tempered work. . . . Work that comes out of guilt and fear and want and all those phantoms your generation is very happy to be without. And you sit there with that stupid transcendental grin on your face and say it's irrelevant.

ANDY: Save it, Dad. Save it for some other stupid sod. One of the ninety-nine per cent. No point in wasting it on me. I'm one of the chosen. That's right, isn't it? Anyway, it's all relative.

GEORGE: What?

ANDY: It's all relative.

GEORGE: Which particular revolutionary handbook did you pick that one up from? Or is that Dave? It isn't all relative. Some things are absolute. Humbug is absolute. Rubbish is absolute. Sloppy, sentimental and worthless. And waste. And it is a bloody waste. You'll end up like our friend, upstairs stripping wardrobes for a living. (*To receiver.*) What? Yes. But I've been holding on for the last ten minutes. I *did* ring earlier. Half an hour ago. What? How do you mean too late? When I rang before you said it was too early. Now you say it's too late. How do . . . well, whose fault is it? Of course it's your fault. Oh . . . get stuffed.
(GEORGE'*s indignation is spread between the operator and* ANDY.)
Words fail me. They always do in the end. Worst method of communicating with anybody. Sorry.

ANDY: Come on, Dad, we have a laugh, don't we?

GEORGE (*shouting upstairs*): There's no taxi. I'll go and try and catch one down the road. Be ready.
(POLLY *comes down almost at the same moment as* GEORGE *is putting on his coat.*)
(*To* ANDY.) Sorry.

POLLY: What was that?

ANDY: The *Oxford English Dictionary* triumphs again.
(GEOFF *comes downstairs.*)
(ANDY *goes upstairs.*)

(POLLY *is all dressed up, ready.*)

POLLY: Nice?

GEOFF: Very nice.

POLLY: Can you do this?

(GEOFF *begins to fasten her ear-rings on.*)

(ANDY *returns for some milk.*)

ANDY: Excuse me. Sorry to interrupt.

POLLY: He's only doing my ear-rings, love.

GEOFF: He knows?

POLLY: No. Anyway. No. He's been having a set-to with George. Where are you off to tonight?

GEOFF: Nowhere.

POLLY: Nowhere?

GEOFF: No.

POLLY: You could stop here and watch George on the telly if you wanted.

GEOFF: No. Is Brian going to this thing tonight?

POLLY: Who?

GEOFF: Brian.

POLLY: I suppose so. It's a duty do. M.P.s and their ladies. You call him Brian?

(POLLY *should embark on some job at this point entirely out of keeping with her get up. Dusting or cleaning up or polishing.*)

GEOFF: Why not?

POLLY: What does he call you?

GEOFF: Doesn't call me anything.

POLLY: Do you think he fancies you?

GEOFF: Have you seen the chuck? (*He is clearing up his tools.*)

POLLY: The what?

GEOFF: For the drill.

POLLY: He probably does. What does it look like? Have you ever been in bed with a man?

GEOFF: Come on. Everybody has some time or other.

POLLY: Have they? James had it somewhere this morning. George hasn't.

GEOFF: Not bed, but at school. As a kid. Something, there must have been.

POLLY: What I said, but he says not. That's his generation for

63

you. Things used to be different. More fraught. Is this it?

GEOFF: And now he's too old to start. Lend us that. I'll sweep up.

POLLY: But you can tell Brian fancies you, the way he never talks to you.

GEOFF: You'll get all mucky.

POLLY: Don't you think so?

GEOFF: Maybe, maybe. And if he does, then?

POLLY: Nothing. Do you know when someone fancies you?

GEOFF: You tell me.

POLLY: You told me.

GEOFF: What're you after?

POLLY: Nothing. Just interested. Has he touched you? Brian. He's very well off.

GEOFF: Do me a favour. Ask him, why don't you? If you're so keen. Get it all mapped out. I'm only part-time here, you know.

POLLY: Sorry. Well, stop fiddling about and talk to me.

(*He is about to kiss her, when the taxi hoots outside and* GEORGE *is heard coming in.*)

GEORGE: Come on. Geoff, we'll have to drop you at Oxford Circus, there's not time to go your way.

(*He opens the stairs door and shouts, only* ANDY *is either just coming down or has been behind the door all the time.*)

We're going now. I don't know what time we'll be back. Damn. I never rang Enid. She was going to the hospital today.

POLLY: There isn't time now, love. Switch the programme on, you're missing it. And make sure James does a pee. Your supper's in the oven.

(*They go.*)

(ANDY *switches on the set. He gets something from the fridge. Cake, or a mixture of unsuitable food which he puts beside him on the sofa without a plate. The television warms up. He tries several channels before* GEORGE *appears.*)

GEORGE (TV): Somehow society ought always to be kept open. There must be a choice. Until you give people a choice there will always be people going up society by the wrong ladders ... sex, fashion, crime.

VOICE (TV): But you say there must be options. What I don't understand is what changes you would make in the State System as it exists today.

GEORGE (TV): Look, I am a product of the State System and admirable though it may be in some respects in others it is appalling.

VOICE (TV): Appalling.

GEORGE (TV): But it isn't education simply. You see, I believe that some people are better than others, better not because they're cleverer or more cultivated or God knows . . . (*he laughs*) because they're better off. But because they're more . . . more human. I used to believe that the relation between such people and education was one of cause and effect . . .

(ANDY *who has been watching it for a long time with his hand on the switch either switches it off or switches it over. He takes a long swig from the milk bottle and switches it off altogether as the lights fade briefly, and go up again on* GEORGE, BRIAN *and* POLLY, *sat round the kitchen table.*)

GEORGE: It's autumn. Autumn. The start of term. The real beginning of the year. I've always kept terms, ever since I was five years old. Autumn when you moved up a class, changed teachers, got a new exercise book. New satchel, school socks. I even went into the army in September. And Oxford in October, trunks in the lodge, leaves down Parks Road. Track suits. And now Parliament again. Still in terms.

There are people whose year begins with the Calendar. Begins, as Fleet Street decrees it should begin, with travel brochures and sales in Oxford Street. How many? Most people, I suppose. Wish class away there would still be this: we are two nations because our years have different bones. Terms are part of the crumbling skeleton of the Christian year. Advent, annunciation, birth, passion and pentecost.

Our year begins as theirs does. Theirs . . . whose? The masses. The people. The voters. I was in America a year on a scholarship. After Oxford. There were no terms there. It was time with the stays taken out of it, no rhythm to the calendar, no Christian holidays, no Easter or Whitsuntide. A secular state. There were sudden holidays in the middle of nowhere. Like missing a step on a stair. Lincoln's birthday. Labour Day. Odd, capricious. I like ceremony. I like pattern.

(*The lights go up as he addresses these last remarks to his wife and* BRIAN.)

Perhaps I am a Christian. Perhaps that's what's wrong with me. Or boredom.

POLLY: If you're so bored you could put the milk bottles out.

BRIAN: Boredom at least implies there's something better.

(GEORGE *does put the milk bottles out.* POLLY *is referring to a printed list, getting together some clothes. She holds up a little pink blazer.*)

POLLY: Look at his little jacket. Doesn't it look pretty?

GEORGE: How much is this Greyfriars Trousseau going to cost?

POLLY: Nothing. It's coming out of Aunt Betty's money.

(GEORGE *fingers a waspish football jersey.*)

GEORGE: I particularly resent money spent on kitting him out for competitive games.

POLLY: All games are competitive.

GEORGE: How's he going to get to the flaming school, with the streets thick with sex maniacs.

POLLY: They have a rota. I've got into a group. It's Thursdays our day.

GEORGE: Thus dragging us willy-nilly into association with all the other educational queue jumpers. If there's one thing I don't fancy at nine o'clock in the morning it's chauffeuring round a cartload of Jasons and Jeremys.

POLLY: Half-past eight.

GEORGE: Cash name tapes. They were always great dividers. Like three initials. What's this?

POLLY: His hair.

GEORGE: All this?

POLLY: It says they prefer it short.

GEORGE: Short? (*He runs upstairs.*) It's not a flaming monastery.

POLLY: You all right, love?

(BRIAN *nods.*)

It's all show is this. Andy's the one. Now he's back at school what does it matter.

BRIAN: He *is* back?

POLLY: Never left. It was all talk. In this house it generally is. You have to take it all with a piece of cake.

GEORGE: He looks like a little lavatory brush. I wonder are there any other alterations to the fabric the school requires. Eyelashes clipped to regulation length? Circumcision perhaps?

POLLY: If he doesn't mind, I don't.

BRIAN: Anyway, all games are not competitive.

POLLY: All competitive games are.

GEORGE: Yes. I suppose now we've seen him safely on to the escalator you'll start worrying about Elizabeth. Already at five more eccentric than Edith Sitwell ever was. I wonder whether there's a handily situated atheist convent?

POLLY: I shouldn't worry. She'll probably slump into marriage same way as I did. I was a bright girl, you know.

GEORGE: You were not a bright girl. You talked like a man and you smoked cigars. That is not intellect.

POLLY: I was brighter than anybody else in my year.

GEORGE: And where are they now, your year? Gossip columnists on the *Evening Standard*, publishers' readers, hostesses on late-night television programmes, the commanding heights of the economy. You're well out of it.

POLLY: I ought to say at this juncture that since I didn't manage to get to Sainsbury's there is nothing for supper.

GEORGE: Eggs?

POLLY: No.

GEORGE: Can't you raid the store cupboard?

POLLY: Yes, if you fancy gooseberries on toast. Couldn't we go out?

GEORGE: No sitters. Incidentally, Geoff rang when you were out.

POLLY: Geoff? What about?

GEORGE: Nothing much. Talk. He hasn't been round for a bit, has he? I've not seen him anyway.

POLLY: If you can think of anything else for him to do. I can't.

GEORGE: I'd just got used to him. I quite like him. He said he might come round.

POLLY: Here? When?

GEORGE: Any time. Tonight, I suppose.

POLLY: What time?

GEORGE: Didn't say. Doesn't matter, we're not going out.

POLLY: I was just thinking could we not go out? To eat.

GEORGE: How can we? Why do you suddenly want to go out, anyway? There'll be enough meals out starting tomorrow. Why
do we have to eat at all? Couldn't we just give it a miss?

POLLY: I suppose you're bored with eating now?

GEORGE: Yes. In at one end of the tunnel and out the other.

POLLY: Shall we go out or shan't we?

BRIAN: Don't bother about me. I don't mind one way or the
other.

POLLY: I didn't have any lunch. We haven't been out for ages.
(*Pause.*)

GEORGE: No. Look. Why don't I go out to the Koh-I-Noor and
fetch some? Then you won't have to do anything.

POLLY: It's not that . . . all right.
(GEORGE *goes out.*)
Oh, God. Why is it always me that gets the tap end of the
bath?
(POLLY *puts the oven on.* BRIAN *says nothing.*)
Have *you* seen Geoff?

BRIAN: Have I seen him?

POLLY: You do see him, don't you?

BRIAN. Yes. Sometimes.

POLLY: Sometimes. I wondered whether that was what you were
glum about.

BRIAN: No. Oh, no.

POLLY: Because he's going away. Did you know that?

BRIAN: Yes.

POLLY: Do you know where?

BRIAN: Yes.

POLLY: Where?

BRIAN: Torremolinos.

POLLY: What to do?

BRIAN: He has this friend who's opening a restaurant.

POLLY: Another friend. So. There we are.

BRIAN: What? Oh. Yes.

POLLY: Don't you want to know how I found out?

68

BRIAN: Found out what?

POLLY: You and Geoff.

BRIAN: It wasn't that much of a secret.

POLLY: You never told me.

BRIAN: No, I suppose not.

POLLY: He started wearing your after-shave lotion.

BRIAN: You can buy it in shops. I don't have it specially blended.

POLLY: That and . . . vibes.

BRIAN: Vibes.

POLLY: You can tell you knew each other better than you let on.

BRIAN: Not much better. He's still a bit of a mystery to me.

POLLY: So in the end I asked him point-blank. And he told me.

BRIAN: Yes. He told me he told you. He may be coming round
       later on to collect his stuff.

POLLY: He didn't tell me.

BRIAN: He told me about you.

POLLY: He didn't tell me about you. Why is that, I wonder?

BRIAN: He knew I wouldn't mind. In my situation one can't really
       afford to. I was . . . a bit shocked about you.

POLLY: Shocked. You were shocked? What had you to be shocked
       about?

BRIAN: Polly, you are married.

POLLY: Yes. But I loved him.
       (*Pause.*)
       No, I didn't. Did you?

BRIAN: No.

POLLY: Did he love you?

BRIAN: Oh, no. He obliges, but he's not that way, anyway.

POLLY: But it's a good job I didn't love him. Otherwise I should
       have been a bit, you know, cross.

BRIAN: Cross. What a funny word.

POLLY: I should have had a right to be cross.

BRIAN: It's like a French farce. I go out one door, you come in at
       the other.

POLLY: I suppose this is what's meant by talking it over like grown
       up people, i.e. neither of us could care a damn.

BRIAN: I care. He wasn't in love with you, though?

POLLY: No. What did he talk about to you?

69

BRIAN: Questions mainly. Lots of questions.

POLLY: What about?

BRIAN: Anything. What did I think of President Kennedy. Had there been a plot. Would there be another war. Had I ever spoken to the Prime Minister.

POLLY: Yes, that's it. That's like it was with me.

BRIAN: And looking for a way in, somehow. As if it were all to do with being clued up. Question and answer, but not to any purpose.

POLLY: And you can't put him off, can you. He gets moody. I know I wasn't much help. I got a bit bored.

BRIAN: I wasn't bored. I felt . . . a bit sorry for him.

POLLY: I didn't.

BRIAN: You're not coming out of this very well.

POLLY: Did you smoke with him?

BRIAN: I don't smoke. Oh *smoke*. No. No. He asked me. I wouldn't.

POLLY: I did.

BRIAN: Nice?

POLLY: No. Made it less boring. I was sick once. Just like having a baby. 'Course I've seen more of him than you. Perhaps you'd have got bored. Except that was what I wanted really, a good boring man. George is so interesting all the time it gets boring. Whereas having a boring man was rather interesting.

BRIAN: I don't think you were all that well suited.

POLLY: What about . . . sex?

BRIAN: It was actually quite a bit before we got on to sex.

POLLY: Do you know, I found that. I think these days it seems to come quite low down on the list. There's a good deal of . . . I don't know . . . well just cuddles.

BRIAN: Yes.

POLLY: I find that a bit disturbing.

BRIAN: Do you? It's what they like. It's one of the differences nowadays. I've noticed it before.

POLLY: Why don't they get on with it, do you think?

BRIAN: They . . . are . . . the young . . . him, Andy . . . nicer than we were, I reckon. I think things are different. Drifting, not pushing. Accepting.

POLLY: You?

BRIAN: Me, I suppose. Things in general. Not . . . not scoring. And it's not pot. It's them. And it's admirable. I wish it were me.

POLLY: He said I was very warm. Didn't he say that to you?

BRIAN: No. He said . . . no. He didn't say that.

POLLY: I suppose I am rather warm, really. George says I'm warm. You never know, do you?

BRIAN: What?

POLLY: *You* do, I suppose. But what you're like. Until there's been someone else, and there never was, you see—so I didn't know I was warm . . . anything . . . I thought that was just George. But now there's been someone else, I suppose, I must be. And you find you're something else besides. Someone else he, George, doesn't know, and now I've got to go back to being just what I was. And it's going to be so . . . (*she is crying*) boring.

(ANDY *is heard coming down the stairs and* POLLY *quickly switches on her transistor.*)

ANDY: What's up?

POLLY (*above the music, which is very loud and martial, say Sousa*): Nothing, love. (*She blows her nose.*) I'm just affected by the music.

ANDY: Is it George?

POLLY: Dad? No. Honestly. Is it, Brian?

BRIAN: No. We were just having a jolly good cry together. It's our age, you know.

ANDY: What's happened to all the food?

POLLY: George has just gone out for something. Look in the store cupboard if there's anything you fancy.

(ANDY *looks and comes out with a bottle of gooseberries, which he opens and begins spooning them out, occasionally drinking the juice from the bottle.*)

ANDY: You're sure you're all right?

POLLY: Positive. Honestly.

(*They sit in awkward silence for a bit while* ANDY *spoons in the gooseberries, and they watch him.*)

ANDY: Good these are.

71

POLLY: Good. They're last year's. This year they were nothing at all. (*To* BRIAN.) Nothing at all.

BRIAN: Were they?

POLLY: Nothing. Greenfly.

(*She still sniffs silently.*)

ANDY (*to* BRIAN): Do you want any?

BRIAN: No. I . . . No.

(*Knock at the door.*)

POLLY (*leaping up*): That'll be Geoff.

(*She runs very quickly upstairs.* ANDY *shrugs and answers the door.*)

GEOFF: How do.

ANDY: She's upstairs. You know Brian?

(GEOFF *raises hand to* BRIAN.)

GEOFF: I called round to collect the rest of my gear.

ANDY (*through stairs door*): Mum. Geoff. Do you know where it all is?

GEOFF: More or less.

(ANDY *sits down again, goes on with the gooseberries. The silence is still pretty awkward.*)

ANDY: Gooseberry?

GEOFF: What?

ANDY: Home-made. (*Holding out bottle.*)

GEOFF: No, thanks. No, O.K., I will. (*He tries one.*) You seen my set-square?

ANDY: In James's box, try.

(GEORGE *now appears with two carriers and several silver foil cartons of Indian food, which he dumps on the kitchen table.*)

GEORGE: Hello, stranger. We were just saying you'd not been round. You staying for supper?

GEOFF: No.

GEORGE: Indian food. There's always plenty.

ANDY: Except for the Indians.

GEOFF: I'll see to it, shall I?

GEORGE: Would you?

(GEOFF *puts food in oven, etc.*)

Drink? (*To* BRIAN.) No? No.

(GEOFF *has now got most of his gear together.*)

72

Are you going?

GEOFF: Yes.

BRIAN: To Spain.

GEORGE: Spain?

GEOFF: I'd borrowed one or two books. I don't know where they go.

GEORGE: Take some more if you want.

GEOFF: I'd better not. It'll be a bit before I'm back.

GEORGE: Whereabouts?

GEOFF: Torremolinos . . . I'm going to help set up this restaurant.

GEORGE: Torremolinos?

GEOFF: Yeah. It's good-bye to The Smoke. Anywhere.

(GEOFF *is putting the books back on the shelf.*)

GEORGE: Take some. It's not exactly Wittenberg, Torremolinos.

GEOFF: What? I can never follow you.

ANDY: It wouldn't suit him so he can't see why it should suit you either.

GEORGE: I just don't think Torremolinos Public Library will be much cop.

ANDY: I envy you. I wish it were me.

GEOFF: I don't know what to choose.

ANDY: Here. I'll choose some.

GEOFF (*to* ANDY): I had a tape measure. Have you seen it . . .

GEORGE: It's on the sink. I shouldn't worry about books, Geoff. Books are on their way out, nowadays, didn't you know that? Words are on their last legs. Words, print and also thought. That's also for the high jump. The sentence, that dignified entity with subject and predicate, is shortly to be made illegal. It probably already is in Torremolinos. Wherever two or three words are gathered together, you see, there is grave danger that thought might be present. All assemblies of words will be forbidden, in favour of patterns of light, videotape, every man his own telecine. Oh, and vibes. Yes, vibes. Does she know you're here?

GEOFF: A lot of the time I never understand what you're saying.

(GEORGE *goes upstairs for* POLLY.)

ANDY: You're not missing much. Mum.

GEORGE: You'll wake the kids. I'll get her.

F

(POLLY *comes downstairs.*)

POLLY: You're going then?

GEOFF: Yes.

POLLY: Is there anything you want?

GEOFF: No.

ANDY: Cheers.

POLLY: Where you going?

ANDY: Only out.

(*Goes out by outside door.* ANDY *should sense he is spare before going.* GEOFF *is left with* BRIAN *and* POLLY.)

GEOFF: Well, I'm off.

POLLY: Oh, are you off?

GEOFF: Yes. I'd better. Not mad, are you?

BRIAN: Me? No.

POLLY: No.

GEOFF: My fault really.

POLLY: You don't want a cup of tea?

GEOFF. No. Something I wanted to say. It . . . it wasn't sex. I mean, it was. I wasn't after anything, but it's the least part of it. Nobody ever explains to you how the system works, what the timetable is, sort of. There ought to have been somebody when I was . . . I don't know . . . somebody to say, "Look, this is the last bus. If you're not on this one you're going to have to walk."

(POLLY *remembers something he has left and is about to give it to him.*)

No. Have that. We're free-loaders people like me. Hitch-hiking. Whereas you . . . all you . . . you're on the motorway. We're other routes. We're . . . we're lumbered.

(GEOFF *goes leaving* POLLY *and* BRIAN *rather lost.*)

(GEORGE *comes back.*)

GEORGE: Geoff gone?

POLLY: Mmm.

GEORGE: I wanted to say good-bye. I shall miss him, you know. I'd got quite to like him. Wasted, you know a boy like that. Wasted. He was quite bright. He's somebody in the dustbin. Torremolinos.

POLLY: He'll be all right. He's beautiful. He won't be in the dustbin for long. He's got his head screwed on right.

GEORGE: No. You don't see it, Polly. You think because he's pretty and knows a Chesterfield when he sees it that he's got a pretty nice life. But I tell you, it's waste. It's like Dickens. Fortunes in the dust heap. How do we cast the net wider or make it with a finer mesh? Or are nets what we want? Somehow you see society's got to be kept open. We can't afford to lose people. Somehow boys like that . . .

POLLY: Shut up.

GEORGE: What?

POLLY: One thing about Geoff . . .

GEORGE: Why?

POLLY: Just for once, let it pass. Shut up. No comment. You always have to fetch everything down to words.

GEORGE: What else would you prefer . . . the music programme?

POLLY: Nowhere, there's nowhere safe . . . from words with you. No . . . no secret room, but what you have to be in there like an auctioneer's clerk, cataloguing, describing, relating, reducing everything to a collection of objects, sticking labels on them. Lot numbers. And though nothing's been changed, nothing taken away, just listed, catalogued and explained . . . yet it's less. You make it less, George. It's not a place any more.

GEORGE: It just happens that all I was saying was . . . Geoff is a very good example of something . . .

POLLY: He isn't an *example*. That's it. Can't you see? Always this is what it's like. It's as if this or as if that. No. This is what it is. There isn't a gap. You don't have to be describing always. Not for me, anyway. Just leave it. Don't say it. (*She is crying*.) All your talk, and you see less than anybody else. You can't even see what's under your nose.

GEORGE: Like what?

POLLY: Like . . . Oh, Georgie . . . I don't know . . . like what people are . . . I don't know . . . like . . .

GEORGE: Like?

POLLY: You're the dead one, George. Irony, litotes, zeugma . . . that's all you are. Just a figure of speech.

(BRIAN *gets up*.)

75

GEORGE: Don't go, please.

BRIAN: No, actually I'd better go.

GEORGE (*to Polly*): Look. What is all this about? What am I supposed to have done?

POLLY: Nothing. Nothing.

GEORGE: Nothing. Right. (*As if that settles it.*) And what about you?

BRIAN: Me?

GEORGE: You're not exactly Nancy with the Laughing Face. Will one of you tell me what I'm supposed to have done?

BRIAN: You? You've done nothing. Look. There is something I ... well, I ought to explain before tomorrow. Remember those postcards?

GEORGE: Ignore them ... it's ... forget about them ...

BRIAN: No. Something else has happened since then.

ENID'S VOICE: Hello!

(BRIAN *gets up hurriedly.*)

POLLY: Oh, Christ. That's all it wanted. No, stay.

BRIAN: No, I'll nip out ...

(ENID *puts her head round the door.*)

ENID: Coming, hiddy, or not.

GEORGE: Now then.

ENID: Cheer up, dear. I'm not stopping. I've got a taxi waiting.

POLLY: Taxi? Where to?

ENID: Stanmore, where else?

POLLY: That'll cost the earth.

ENID: No. It won't, you see, because ...

GEORGE: What's happened about your tests?

ENID: That's what I called in to say. I've been living in fear and trembling and eventually screwed up my courage to the sticking point—Hello, Mr. Thing, didn't see you there— went to see dirty Doctor Proctor who, of course, has had the results for a week and never bothered to tell me.

GEORGE: And what is it?

ENID: Nothing at all. I'm all right. I said what about the shadow and he said well that's all it was, a shadow, no substance to it at all. (*To* BRIAN.) Sorry to visit all this on you.

(BRIAN *should go upstairs.*)

76

GEORGE: Oh, Enid. (*Kisses her.*)

ENID: I really thought it was the fell sergeant this time. I made my will, everything, and such a weep doing it.

POLLY: Enid, you are a twerp.

ENID: Twerp! I thought it was curtains.

GEORGE: I did.

ENID: Did you? I'm glad you didn't tell me. Anyway, all gone. So I went to my class tonight the first time for three weeks. And Zoë and I went out for a little celebration with the male model who turns out to be a taxi-driver in his spare time and not a nancy at all. He says it's coming from Leeds. They all talk like that. You all right, dear?

POLLY: Yes. 'Course I'm all right.

GEORGE: And how do you feel?

ENID: At this moment, dear, a bit tiddly. Sure?

POLLY: Yes.

ENID: I suppose it ought to teach me to mend my ways. But I can't see how. George dear, would you do something for me. Go along to the end and get me some ciggies. It's for Gerry. He's been ever so good.

GEORGE: I've got some here. He could have those.

ENID: No, dear, those aren't the sort he likes.

GEORGE: Well, what sort?

ENID: Oh, any sort. He's not fussy. Off you go before they close.
 (POLLY *and* ENID *are alone.*)
 You been crying, dear?

POLLY: No.

ENID: What about?

POLLY: Nothing. I haven't.

ENID: Last time I saw you crying . . .

POLLY: I haven't been.

ENID: . . . was when you were fifteen. Over Michael Fitton.

POLLY: Who?

ENID: Michael Fitton, dear, don't you remember? A funny boy with weak ankles who played the violin and lived in the Drysdales.

POLLY: That's right. With ginger hair.

ENID: He's gone to New Zealand. I saw his mother in McCorquo-

77

dales last week. You wouldn't think there'd be openings for violinists in New Zealand, would you? She said they were crying out for them.

POLLY (*crying*): Oh, Mum. You are lovely.

ENID: Then there was Roger Mowbray. He stood for the council this year.

POLLY: His . . . his feet used to smell.

ENID: Terrible. Probably still do. He didn't get in anyway. That was a narrow escape, too. You were quite smitten with him.

POLLY: I never was.

ENID: Yes, you were. You've forgotten, but you were. I remember Leonard saying.

(*Pause.*)

Is it that young man?

POLLY (*still crying*): Sort of, I suppose. Oh dear. Things altogether, really. Things going on. And on. This is the way things are going to be now.

ENID: Blow your nose, dear.

POLLY: The family's complete, we don't want any more. . . . If I had another baby I think George would strangle it . . . and then him.

ENID: Who?

POLLY: George . . . George is . . . like he is . . . And this is our hand. It's been dealt and now all there is to do is to play it for, what? Thirty years.

ENID (*she is smoking*): Thirty years.

POLLY: You don't smoke.

ENID: Oh, I do occasionally. Special occasions.

(*Pause.*)

You wonder sometimes how you land up where you do. I look across at Leonard sometimes on a night and think of myself running up the steps of the Slade all those years ago. Only it doesn't seem all those years ago. I thought life was going to be like Brahms, do you know? Instead it's, well it's been Eric Coates. And very nice, too. But not Brahms.

POLLY: You and Dad have been very happy I've always thought.

ENID: Oh, yes, it's been very happy.

POLLY: I've got so much left. Spare. I suppose I ought to be more

78

like you and further education.

ENID: Going to classes? Oh, no, that's not the answer, classes. Don't start on that. I've been to so many classes. Pottery classes, first aid classes, classes in bookbinding and the first principles of Economics. Keats. Yoga. Poland ... Cockpit of Europe. Judaism, an Introduction to Flower Arrangement. Classes in primary schools and scout huts, vestries in the black-out, sat there with my pencil and pad, improving my-self, leaving Leonard's supper ready. Making contact, taking up the slack, such an awful lot of slack left to take up some-how. Like a pie, marriage, so much pastry sliced off the dish. Oh, no, don't start on that. That's not the answer.

POLLY: Did you have any affairs?

ENID: One or two. At least I suppose that's what they were. You never know, do you? I'm supposed to offer advice, aren't I? Your silly old mother. I'm not much good as Evelyn Home.

POLLY: I'm better for the cry, it's all right.

ENID: People ask you for help and all you do is root about in your own trunk trying to come across something similar.

POLLY: It's all right.

ENID: I wouldn't tell him.

POLLY: No? I wanted to.

ENID: It's like setting him a test. No. Marriage isn't Outward Bound, dear. Keep it to yourself, if he doesn't know.

POLLY: No. He doesn't know.

ENID: Stop talking now. Or I shall get on your nerves.

POLLY: No.

ENID: Yes. The trouble with both of us, dear, is that we've both been hit with the doolally stick.

GEORGE (*coming in*): Hit with what.

ENID: The doolally stick. A bit daft, it means, the pair of us, your wife and I.

(*Taxi hoots.*)

That's Gerry. He's taking me all the way back to Stanmore for nothing. He's lovely. Is everything all right?

GEORGE: Champion, champion.

ENID (*kisses* POLLY): 'Bye, dear. I'm afraid you've got your old mother for another few years yet.

79

POLLY: Enid. (*And for the first time kisses her with genuine affection.*)

(BRIAN *reappears.*)

(*Taxi hoots.*)

That's Gerry again. So impatient. Toodloo.

GEORGE: That's some good news, anyway.

POLLY: Is it?

BRIAN: I wondered . . . Anyway, I'll be off.

GEORGE: What is it, for Christ's sake? I can't see why you worry about it? It is that, isn't it? The postcards.

BRIAN: No. No. That's to say, whoever it is has obviously got a bit tired of the situation. I'm still not certain what I'm going to do. He . . . has sent . . . they must have saved the clipping . . . from the newspaper. And sent it to my agent.

GEORGE: So what's happened?

BRIAN: Blessington, my agent, is an admirable man, who puts down half a bottle of whisky a day and has two convictions for drunken driving, but otherwise a pillar of society. With three teenage sons. The upshot is he has made some inquiries, and, as he put it, sounded opinion in the constituency and . . . I am not going to be asked to stand again.

GEORGE: But that's monstrous.

POLLY: They can't do that, can they, just chuck you out in between elections?

BRIAN: No. Not now. Not straight away, not without there being a fuss.

GEORGE: You can sit it out. There's three years at least before they can shift you.

BRIAN: It all depends. I can say, you see, I want to devote more time to business. That's an eminently respectable reason.

GEORGE: The sods. When you consider that there are many Members of Parliament, and alas not merely in the Conservative Party, men who have never had a moment of self doubt in their lives. We don't expel them for greed, for arrogance, for debating the state of the nation in voices that would get them thrown out of a saloon bar, for spending lunchtime in strip clubs or trundling their throbbing pink tools round to little blondes in Victoria. What is it in this particular sin?

POLLY: What are you going to do?

BRIAN: If I give up, you mean?

GEORGE: You mustn't give up.

BRIAN: Go back full time to the works, I can. Couldn't do that if there were a hullabaloo, you see. And it's a bit late to strike out.

POLLY: You could always do social work.

BRIAN. What?

POLLY: Some sort of social work.

BRIAN: Me? Can you see it? Expiate my sin stroke crime by picking old men off bomb sites and feeding them tea and wads in some East End church hall. Along with a lot of other damp young men, fugitives from teachers' training colleges, ex-altar boys, schizophrenics going straight and High Church young men who make daring jokes about vestments. The lame ducks. The ones who brought a note. No, thank you.

GEORGE: You're going to fight it?

BRIAN: I may do. I may not. I haven't thought it out yet. I only got to know this morning.

GEORGE: It's blackmail.

BRIAN: That's right, it's blackmail. But don't get worked up about it.

GEORGE: Worked up, Christ!

BRIAN: Some people might reckon I'm half a man. But then so are you, George, in a different way. So are all politicians. Come close and you'll see a scar. We've all had an operation. We've been seen to, doctored, like cats. Some essential part of our humanity has been removed. It's not honesty or straightforwardness, or the usual things politicians are supposed to lack. It's a sense of the ridiculous, the bloody point-lessness of it all, that's what they've lost. They think they're important. As if it mattered.

GEORGE: Now. Has he put anything down on paper?

BRIAN: Who?

GEORGE: Your agent.

BRIAN: He wrote me a letter.

GEORGE: Saying what?

BRIAN: Saying what I told you.

GEORGE: Outright? Not just hints or . . .

BRIAN: Hints! He gave the actual date of the newspaper.

GEORGE: Then you've got him. Where is it?

BRIAN: What?

GEORGE: Because if he actually committed himself on paper.

BRIAN: I threw it away.

GEORGE: What? But you only have to show that letter . . .

BRIAN: I don't want to show that letter to anybody.

GEORGE: But there's a principle.

BRIAN: George. Fuck principle. I wasn't going to say anything because I knew we'd have to have all this to go through. Just keep out of it. Smashing, isn't it? A lively little liberal scuffle. A nice straightforward battle between right on the left and wrong on the right. Where you can go in with fists flying and hang the consequences.

GEORGE: I know it's harder for you to see it, but . . .

BRIAN: No, I see it. A clear issue. Vermin. The Tory beast. The old ogre of intolerance as it still stalks the constituencies. That's how she fits in, that dog woman, Mrs. Boothroyd.

POLLY: Brodribb.

BRIAN: A target a mile wide and all stupid. Safe enough there, George.

GEORGE: That's balls. Whoever it was it's monstrous. You can't think it's just that.

BRIAN: Not just, though that's part of it. You'd like a good fight, wouldn't you, George?

GEORGE: Yes, I would. It's a scandal.

BRIAN: It's a scandal. And they're pretty hard to come by, aren't they, situations where there isn't something to be said on both sides? No balance. No assessment needed. No. That's what you're missing and you'd enjoy it too much. Something really solid to fetch the phrases out, get the life-giving adrenalin flowing. Well, I wouldn't waste them on me. Save them for the old age pensioners.

GEORGE: Brian.

BRIAN: No offence, George. I appreciate it. Night, love. (*He kisses* POLLY.)
(*Exits.*)

82

GEORGE: He's worked up about it now. I'll go after him.

POLLY: No.

GEORGE: But he's wrong. He must put up a fight about it. It's years ago. My God if they can do that . . . he'll come round. I mean. What do you think? It's pathetic.

POLLY: There've probably been other times.

GEORGE: Have there? Not that anybody knows about. Anyway, what if there have. These days. It's nothing. Nothing. Blessington.

POLLY: Bassington.

GEORGE: I'd like an electric device to send a short sharp shock through the arses of men like that. And when was it, 1955, '56. Fifteen years ago. Five minutes with a soldier in the park. Jesus Christ. What is there in that that makes him unfit to represent the people. What next, it makes you wonder, nose picking?

(POLLY *slips out during this speech, crying.*)

"It has come to our notice that in March 1953 in the course of a week-end at the Hyde Park Hotel on three separate occasions and notwithstanding there was a lavatory only a few yards down the corridor, you nevertheless took it upon yourself to piss in the basin. This, taken in conjunction with the fact that you have frequently failed to change your under-wear twice daily has raised grave doubts as to your suitability to continue to represent this constituency and the committee has therefore decided that . . ."

(*He finds he is alone. He sits down on the sofa, silent and jaded. He begins to get ready for bed. Unbuttons his shirt, puts out some of the lights. Faintly, as ever, music upstairs.*)

(ANDY *comes in through the outside door.*)

ANDY: George.

GEORGE: Hello.

ANDY: S'Mam?

GEORGE: Bed, I think. Been out?

ANDY: Yep. Geoff go?

(GEORGE *nods.*)

Any food?

GEORGE: In the oven.

(ANDY *goes into kitchen.*)

Better turn it off. And throw away what you don't want.

ANDY: You not eating?

GEORGE: No.

ANDY (*poised with several cartons over the waste bin*): Sure?

GEORGE: No.

(*He drops in the cartons with a thud and a shrug.*)
(*This dumping must be quite explicit and pointed, dumping several cartons distinctly and separately, opening waste bin with his foot each time.*)

ANDY: S'matter?

GEORGE: Tired.

ANDY: Go to bed.

GEORGE: In a minute. She kick you out?

ANDY: Who?

GEORGE: You tell me.

ANDY: No. (*Pause.*) No.

GEORGE: So.

ANDY: I went down the pub.

GEORGE: What for?

(*Pause.*)

ANDY: A drink. Two drinks. Smoke.

GEORGE: Thought you didn't go in for pubs much.

ANDY: Who?

GEORGE: You. Youth. Young people. The younger generation.

ANDY: Us.

GEORGE: Us. That's the big difference. We were never us.

ANDY: I don't feel it.

GEORGE: I didn't then. We'll go down as the last generation before the pill. Still making sly visits to back-street herbalists for the tell-tale pink and purple packets. We . . . I . . . went by train to country stations, Shepreth, Melbourne, Foxton. Distance was still measured in cycle rides, not yet annihilated by the motor car. And with army appetites found out good places to eat. Good meals used to be an achievement then, good restaurants anyway. Not like now, an indulgence, an ordeal or a chore. Then really found reason to welcome Suez. For there we were scattered all over England and suddenly we

84

linked hands and became a generation. By which time I was twenty-eight. Some youth.

ANDY: That's the new period in A levels. Contemporary History from Munich to Suez.

(GEORGE *laughs*.)

GEORGE: Andy.

ANDY: Yes.

GEORGE: I don't mind, you know . . . I go on at you . . . but say, if you wanted to bring anyone back here, you can.

ANDY: No.

GEORGE: You never do.

ANDY: No . . . it's . . . there's never any need.

GEORGE: I don't mind. Polly might. But it's all the same to me whatever you do, really.

ANDY: Thanks.

GEORGE: I mean, to stop if you want them to . . .

ANDY: I knew what you meant. I reckon I'm off to bed.

GEORGE: I suppose that would take some of the fun out of it. Or isn't it fun any more? I suppose you're so cool you never notice. You do have a bird?

ANDY: Sometimes.

GEORGE: That isn't what I meant.

ANDY: Isn't it? You're frightened of getting old, Dad, aren't you? Oh, yes, you are, Dad. You think somehow, Dad, I'm going to supply the vitality. Well, I'm not, Dad. Do you know what your trouble is, Dad?

GEORGE: What's all this Dad business? What's the matter with George all of a sudden?

ANDY: You've stopped looking at things. You don't look and then alter. That's being old, Dad. Not changing any more. So do you want to know something? If you want precise information, I've never been to bed with anybody ever.

GEORGE: I'm sorry.

ANDY: Ever. Have you ever thought what's happened to all the shy people? What's become of them all of a sudden?

GEORGE: Right.

ANDY: Whatever happened to reserve, Dad, and self-consciousness? Was it your government that got rid of guilt? Tell me this,

85

Dad. How is it easier, how is it easier to reach out and touch someone for the first time? Why is it easier for me now, than it was for you then, whenever that was? Because that's the irreducible fact. You envy me, sniffing out what I do, fishing out where I've been, trying to calculate exactly where I've got to in the sexual stakes. Well, listen, Dad, there's nothing to envy yet. You can sleep easy of a night, because I haven't even started.

GEORGE: O.K., O.K.

ANDY: But I tell you this, Dad . . .

(POLLY *comes down in her dressing-gown with transistor.*)

When I do start, and I care, and you say things like that to me, then I shan't simply tell you to mind your own bloody business I shall hit you.

GEORGE: Yes, you do that, *Son* . . . You do that. You're the New Puritans, you lot. Get through the haze of pot and cheap fellowship and underneath you're like everybody else, harsh, censorious bastards.

ANDY: And sometimes, Dad, keep your mouth shut. That's cool. I commend it to you.

(ANDY *goes upstairs.*)

(GEORGE *sits for a moment on the sofa.*)

POLLY: Come on, love, I'm sorry.

GEORGE: What a foul day it's been. All in all.

POLLY: Yes. About Enid. Is she all right, do you think?

GEORGE: Enid? I don't know. I wondered. It seemed funny.

POLLY: Yes, it did.

GEORGE: I can ring that doctor, if you like?

POLLY: No.

GEORGE: Her I care about, don't I?

POLLY: What? Come on, I didn't mean it.

GEORGE: Anyway, if it isn't all right, it must mean . . . there isn't anything to be done. Oh-o-oh. Feel old. And tomorrow it's the new session. A few more years in the cold. Then perhaps a minister for five years, ten if we're lucky. Then I shall be sixty and out. My name to a statute, perhaps, and that's my posterity. That and Andy.

POLLY: And James and Elizabeth.

86

GEORGE: I was a lackey of Transport House. The sum of a small irrelevant career in English public life in the second half of the twentieth century.

POLLY: I wonder, wherever we lived, if we'd be the same? Outside London. East Anglia, say. How do people live there?
(*Pause.*)
Or Truro.

GEORGE (*who has slit open a postal packet containing the local paper sent from the constituency*): Truro?

POLLY: The provinces. Anywhere. People are nicer. Better, anyway. It's London that's wrong.
(*She should retrieve the string and brown paper, tidy to the last, puts it away in a drawer.*)

GEORGE: I was thinking if they'd ever have me back at Oxford we could live in the country all the time. The Cotswolds practically. A lot of them do.

POLLY: Except if we lived outside London, the provinces say, are there people like us. It might be like staying up at Cambridge during the Long Vac. Having to make do with people who were there, whether you liked them or not.

GEORGE: What?

POLLY: Nothing.

GEORGE: Or just come up here at week-ends.

POLLY: London. Come on up.
(POLLY *pauses with hand on light switch as* GEORGE *gets up with the local paper. He sees an item that interests him.*)

GEORGE: That's funny. Do you remember, a long time ago I had a West Indian woman who thought next door were poisoning her cats?

POLLY: No. (*Goes off.*)

GEORGE: I thought she was mad. She wasn't. They were. She's taken them to court and they've been fined.
(GEORGE *switches light off, light streams from stairs door, and he goes upstairs as the curtain comes down.*)